ENDORSEMENTS

In "It's Not Over: You Are Just in the Middle of Your Story", author Buck Marshall crafts a powerful narrative that serves as both a source of inspiration and a guiding light for those navigating the tumultuous waters of personal struggles. This book transcends the typical self-help genre; it acts as a compass, steering readers through their darkest moments and illuminating the path toward healing and hope.

Marshall's writing is infused with authenticity, a quality that stems from his own life experiences. His ability to articulate complex emotions and challenging circumstances suggests a profound understanding of the human condition. Rather than merely presenting theories or platitudes, he shares insights gained from personal battles, allowing readers to feel a genuine connection to his journey. This authenticity is what sets his work apart and makes it resonate deeply with those who may feel lost or overwhelmed.

The narrative is rich with heart, humor, and healing, offering a multifaceted approach to overcoming adversity. Marshall's use of storytelling not only captivates but also empowers readers, inviting them to reflect on their own lives and struggles. Through poignant anecdotes and thoughtful reflections, he illustrates that difficulties are not the end but rather chapters in an expansive narrative that continues to unfold.

Central to the book's message is the concept of resilience. Marshall argues that being in the midst of a challenge does not equate to defeat. Instead, it highlights the importance of perseverance and the belief that a brighter future lies ahead. He encourages readers to embrace their journeys, emphasizing that every setback is an opportunity for growth and transformation.

Filled with wisdom, courage, and incredible insight, "It's Not Over" is an essential read for anyone feeling trapped in a cycle of pain or uncertainty. Marshall's compassionate approach fosters a sense of community and understanding, reminding readers that they are not alone in their struggles. The book serves as a beacon of hope, assuring them that their destiny is still within reach.

In conclusion, Buck Marshall's "It's Not Over: You Are Just in the Middle of Your Story" is more than just a book; it is a lifeline for those seeking direction and solace in their time of need. With its profound insights and heartfelt guidance, it will undoubtedly leave a lasting impact on anyone who dares to open its pages and embark on the journey toward healing and self-discovery.

Bryan Cutshall, Th.D.
President of ISOW Bible College

Buck Marshall's work, "It's Not Over: You're Just in the Middle of Your Story" is a power-packed testament to the strength and goodness of God even when we find ourselves in the meantime. Buck shares from a courageous place of honesty as he shares a meaningful conversation as someone who knows about the struggle to persevere. His voice is a beacon of hope and encouragement. This compelling work tracing the life of Joseph will empower its reader through the Word of God in a confrontational yet heartening appeal to keep going until fulfillment is a reality.

Renee Talley

Dr. Buck Marshall raises the interpretation and application bar on Joseph's up-and-down journey through Scripture. Dr. Marshall gives a smidgen of contrarian and a dash of sweet insight together for a tasty meal of helpful reality. "It's Not Over" is not a "must-read", it is a "should-read" if you want to climb out of your "middle" and into your legacy. I can hardly wait for his next book, there must be more!

Raymond F. Culpepper, D.D.
Executive Director of Division of Care
Church of God, Cleveland, Tennessee

"It's Not Over—You're Just in the Middle of Your Story" by Dr. James Buck Marshall is a book of inspiration and encouragement for anyone who has encountered or is currently walking through a difficult season. Drawing insight from the biblical account of Joseph, this book deepens our understanding of how God can take our darkest moments and shape us into the people of significance He has purposed us to be.

However, this journey is not easy. As Dr. Marshall reveals in each chapter, Joseph faced challenges that we still encounter today. With each challenge comes a lie, a truth, and a corresponding fruit that is beneficial for us to discover. Like Joseph, we have a choice—to buy into the lie evoked by the problem or to hold onto the truth of what God says about it.

Dr. Marshall authentically shares his personal journey of God's shaping hand on his life and ministry. He, like Joseph (as we all must), had to surrender his own expectations and embrace the hope of God's plan. God is a "rewarder of them that diligently seek Him" (Hebrews 11:6b KJV), and this book will encourage you to persevere forward. Beyond your "middle" season, God's promises await!

Rev. Dawn Lipsey
(author of "I Can, I Will"; "Wild, Loud Peace"; and coauthor of "Hope Over Discouragement")

James Buck Marshall delivers a powerful and hope-filled message in "It's Not Over". With wisdom, compassion, personal insight, and some humor, he reminds us that no matter how challenging our current circumstances may seem, they are just one chapter in a much larger story. This book is a timely encouragement for anyone feeling stuck or uncertain, offering the perspective and faith to keep moving forward. Dr. Marshall's words will inspire you to trust that your best days are still ahead.

Dr. Fred Garmon, PhD.
LeaderLabs, Inc.

We are each somewhere along the timeline of our unfinished story. My friend Buck bravely shares his story and in doing so, he draws us all into the truth. THE TRUTH. Father God isn't done by any means. He's just getting started. Wherever the reader finds themselves as they read this honest book, there is truth, encouragement, and healing to be mined on every page. Thank you, Buck—we overcome by the blood of the Lamb and the word of our testimony!

Richard Henderson
Founder
Fellowship of the Sword

Yet those who wait for the Lord will gain new strength; they will mount up with wings like eagles, they will run and not get tired, they will walk and not become weary. Isaiah 40:31 (NASB95)

This verse is the prophetic conclusion that Isaiah asserts in the shadow of the situational, psychological, and spiritual circumstances defined by the previous three verses that outline life and, more pointedly, the life of faith we live as followers of Jesus Christ. Namely: "I have found myself in the middle of cosmic injustice, in the middle of a place where God can't see me, in the middle of a race and I have no 'run' left in me, and in the middle of an exhaustion that has left me unable to 'walk' the path before me!" In response, God speaks through the prophet, "Wait."

We often tend to think that "wait" is surrendering to "stuck" and that stuck is somehow the result of the penalty of my past, and now I am forever suspended there - stuck in "the middle." But irrespective of the path to "the middle" if we will dare to worship God "in the middle," we will find, as the prophet Isaiah declares, He will transform stuck into wait, weakness into strength, and the potential penalty of my past into preparation for promise for my future.

Buck reminds us all, powerfully, poignantly, and personally that this transformation of perspective can only happen "in the middle."

- *In the middle of my storm.*

- *In the middle of my pain.*

- *In the middle of uncertainty.*

- *In the middle of my weakness.*

- *In the middle of my insufficiency.*

"The middle" always holds the threat of becoming "the center". The center of our life. The center of our faith. The center of our purpose. Buck's words frame the certain discovery that the middle is not the center—God is. It is only in "the middle" that we come to terms with what and Who is "the center", and...it is only at that moment we discover that the middle is the intersection between the past behind me and the promise before me and we walk it out "with Him."

If you will, please allow Buck's vulnerable testimony that follows to perhaps become the cup of water that may just quench the parched thirst of a soul trying to trust and hope one more time, in the middle!

Tom Sterbens
Pastor of New Hope Church
Sevierville, TN

Being in the 'middle' of anything can be frustrating or challenging, but when in a spiritual struggle expecting answers, the wait can be excruciating. In 'It's Not Over' Buck Marshall examines this common dilemma through the lens of Scripture, training, and his life experiences, providing uplifting and biblically based encouragement.

Dr. Tony D. Stewart
First Assistant General Overseer
Church of God, Cleveland, TN

IT'S NOT OVER

BUCK MARSHALL

IT'S NOT OVER

You're Just In the Middle of Your Story

Published by Greatness Makers
PO Box 213067, Columbia, SC 29221

www.GreatnessMakers.com

Identifiers:
ISBN: 979-8-9899739-3-4 (paperback)
ISBN: 979-8-9899739-5-8 (hardback)
ISBN: 979-8-9899739-4-1 (ebook)

Available in paperback, hardback, and ebook

Unless otherwise stated, all scriptures are taken from the New American Standard Bible (NASB).

Scriptures marked KJV, AMP, NIV, CEB, ASV, NLT, NASB, and YLT are taken from the King James Version of the Bible, the Amplified Bible, the New International Version, the Common English Version, the American Standard Version, the New Living Translation Bible, the New American Standard Bible, and the Young's Literal Translation of the Holy Bible, respectively.

Any Internet addresses (websites, blogs, etc.) and telephone numbers printed in this book are offered as a resource. They are not intended in any way to be or imply an endorsement by Greatness Makers, nor does Greatness Makers vouch for the content of these sites and numbers for the life of this book.

Editor: Crystal R. Smith

DEDICATION

For Rhea, Caroline, and Jonathan,
the ones who walked every step of this journey with me.
I love you with all my heart.

Table of Contents

FOREWORD

AN INDIVIDUAL'S LIFE HAS a beginning, middle, and end. Sometimes, life is like a comedy, and sometimes, it can seem like a tragedy. Most of the time, life can be like a mystery novel, and while we may hope for a happy ending, we won't know until the final scene plays out.

In literature, the technique of starting a story in the middle is called in medias res, which is a Latin phrase that means "in the middle of things". Rather than starting the story at the beginning, this particular writing technique of beginning in the middle of the action is used to create an often-dramatic opening that seizes the attention of a reader. However, if you're the one living out the story, your attention was captured a long time ago.

The truth is our life story reveals the environment that shaped us and gave us our perspective of the world. Most importantly, our life story can show us how the presence of God has been with us on every page of life's enduring chapters. While our stories are full of precious gems that should be held gently and appreciated for their value, we each have parts of our lives that we deliberately keep hidden from others or don't bring up because we fear others won't want to hear or won't understand. However, we shouldn't bury those treasures but honor them, even those that are the most painful. The painful stories often reveal the two greatest treasures of all: God's providential care and everlasting love.

Just ask Daniel while in the lion's den, Joseph in the pit, and of course, our Lord Jesus on the cross. They were all simply in the middle of their story and the best was yet to come.

Ask Dr. Buck Marshall. His story is Romans 8:28, walking around in shoe leather. "And we know that in all things God works for the good of those who love him, who have been called according to his purpose".

Dr. Marshall's new book will take you on a journey of faith that reveals the core values of trust and commitment. You may find yourself somewhere in his and Rhea's story. If you do, hold on. You're just in the middle, and the finish line of triumph isn't that far away.

Timothy M. Hill

CHAPTER 1

In the Middle of Truth and Lies

Choosing Between Truth and Lies

I T'S NOT OVER. No matter how difficult the circumstances may be, how lonely you feel, how pervasive your fear is, how daunting the obstacles before you, or how devastating the destruction behind you, your story isn't over. Whether you are dealing with devastation from the past, deep wounds from broken relationships, unfulfilled dreams, or deferred hopes, there is still hope for a brighter future. God hasn't forgotten you. He hasn't dropped you off to die in the middle of the wilderness somewhere. Life hasn't dealt HIS plans a fatal blow. He isn't struggling to overcome anyone or anything to fulfill His promise for you. You are just simply...in the middle of your story. Trust me: as I write this, I am in the middle of mine. I will share more about that later.

Real People Facing Real Trials

Christians read the Bible and recognize that the people within it are real individuals. We read their stories and understand these events actually happened, yet sometimes these figures —like Joseph, Bathsheba, David, and Paul—feel more like characters from a Dicken's novel than real people. Their lives can seem more like stories and fables than genuine accounts of someone's journey. This perception is common in the way people view history.

I have read two fascinating historical works. One was Carl Sandburg's multi-volume biography of Abraham Lincoln, and the other was an antique, two-volume set from the early nineteenth century titled *The History of the American War*. On this side of history, we know the war as the American Revolution, but the book was written at the end of the eighteenth century. Both Adams and Jefferson wrote a forward.

I held the leather-bound cotton pages in my hands and read every word. What can be found in these early historical accounts is very different from the current ones. Popular myth attempts to reduce the first and sixteenth Presidents of the United States to simple homogenous caricatures. For example, George Washington *chopped down a cherry tree and couldn't tell a lie*. And another: *Abraham Lincoln freed the slaves and gave his life for the cause*. The problem with relegating them to mythological status is that they lose their humanity, and the reader loses the real story.

In reality, George Washington was challenging to work with and was personally closed off. However, his genius lay in his self-awareness of his role as president, which allowed him to prioritize the country over his own personal advancement. He also elevated those around him based on merit rather than birthright. For instance, Alexander Hamilton would not have risen to power and made a significant impact on the nation had he been limited by the restrictions of the British aristocracy. Moreover, a Broadway musical named *Hamilton* would not exist. As an illegitimate son, Hamilton would not have been given any authority under British rule. However, Washington promoted him because of his remarkable intellect and sagacity.

Abraham Lincoln didn't initially start out wanting to free the slaves. He expressed this during his debates with Stephen Douglas, stating that he wasn't sure they should be free. His primary goal was to limit the expansion of slavery into new territories to avoid the political hotbed that slavery had become. However, as the Civil War unfolded, Lincoln's ability to change his mind became apparent. He eventually came to believe that God was judging the nation for the sin of slavery, declaring that every drop of blood drawn with the lash had to be repaid with blood drawn by the sword. Defying his adviser's council, he drafted the Emancipation Proclamation and fought to secure an amendment to the Constitution.

Both stories seem far more interesting than the *Cherry Tree Washington* or *Abe the Log Splitter* myths. The fact that these were real people who faced challenges and overcame their flaws makes them relatable to Americans, instilling a sense of hope. It's even more essential to grasp the authenticity of the people within the pages of God's Word.

When you consider the common practice of relegating historical figures to fictional characters alongside the tendency of today's Christians to downplay the supernatural aspect of Scripture, you have a problem that can impact eternity. Jack Deere's book *Surprised by the Voice of God* has an excellent chapter entitled "The Problem with the Unreal Bible." Within it, he writes concerning how we have removed the supernatural from our biblical expectations:

> *For many orthodox Christians, the Bible is a book about abstract truths about God rather than a guide into the supernatural realm of God's power. Two sad effects invariably result in reading the Bible in such a de-supernaturalizing manner. First, we experience very little of God's supernatural power. Why? Because we have neither the faith to pray nor the confidence that God can speak to us in any supernatural way. Why do we lack faith? Because our method of reading the Bible has taught us not to expect these things. This leaves us with a moralistic version of Christianity that believes discipline is the key to the spiritual life. Our discipline. Mix that discipline with a little help from God, and it causes us to be better people while we are on our way to heaven. For example, we*

*might study the book of Proverbs and try to
discern principles for raising our children, but
we never learn how to pray with the kind
of faith that delivers a homosexual son from
his homosexuality or a teenage daughter from
drugs. Beyond taking us to heaven, we don't
expect too much from God. And we usually get
what we expect.*[1]

The Bible is a supernatural book written by
supernatural means for supernatural reasons. We should
recognize that this is not merely Aesop's fable, but
rather embrace the supernatural in our lives, viewing the
people within it as real individuals. They were actual
flesh-and-blood people confronting genuine dangers and
challenges. Take your favorite person in the Bible and
stop reading in the middle of their story arc, and you will
find them in the middle of rejection, pain, danger, fear,
doubt, and peril. They were lonely, misunderstood, often
confused, attacked, lied about, and mistreated.

The Bible is a supernatural book written by
supernatural means for supernatural reasons.

They faced lions, giants, armies, moral failures, family
strife, demonic attacks, disease, and more. If you stop
reading in the middle of their story, you might conclude
that God had forsaken them, that He didn't love them,
and that He couldn't keep His promises. However, because
we know the end of their story, we don't often draw

this conclusion. We digest their life stories as ones of victory, miracles, and triumph. Those that lived through it, however, couldn't see the end of their story. And, so, it is with you and me.

If you stop in the middle of your greatest trial to draw conclusions, you might believe that God is limited, powerless, or doesn't care about you. Your life isn't over, so you shouldn't judge it or Him just yet. There is still more to be written, so you must have faith. Too many times, conclusions are drawn on incomplete information. People tend to make permanent decisions based on temporary situations. Believers in Jesus Christ must have an enduring faith that should lead us to respond differently. We must separate the truth from the lies, *including and especially* in the hard times, trusting that God has a purpose and plan. I know it is easier said than done. Fortunately, you don't have to do this alone. The Holy Spirit will empower you to continue believing in God's enduring faithfulness. When life is in severe upheaval, you must have the courage to know it isn't over—you're just in the middle of your story.

> The way you perceive what is happening—either through the lens of deception or truth—will significantly shape your response.

Everyone goes through trials, struggles, and storms. Everyone experiences doubt, fear, and hopelessness. It can't be avoided. The real battle one can affect isn't about difficulties occurring but about believing the truth or the lie amidst those difficulties. In challenging situations, the enemy of your soul tends to exacerbate the problem by trying to convince you that God is to blame; that He's not trustworthy; that it will always be this way; or that there is no hope. He will lie about what has happened, what's going to happen, and even what *is* happening. He will frame the temporary as permanent, God's delay as God's aloofness or judgment, and even redefine the hard times. In other words, he aims to create an image of you being buried and forgotten, covered by a heap of decaying refuse. But consider this: what if, instead, you are being planted? You are placed deep in the earth, nurtured, and given time to germinate, with fertilizer enriching your growth above. You see, the same situation can be framed differently. One is a lie, and one is the truth. The way you perceive what is happening—either through the lens of deception or truth—will significantly shape your response. That's the war you're fighting. That's the war you must win. That's the war that you can win!

Joseph as a Guide

The Bible is replete with examples of powerful men and women of God who went through tough times and came through on the other side. Not only did they survive, but they ended up better off than before their trial. You have the benefit of their experiences, missteps, and lifelong journey. Joseph, the eleventh son of Jacob, is an excellent example of the many different trials we all face today. He is also a great example of how to navigate these tests. He will serve as a guide in the following pages.

God is loving and kind, but we often only see the problems in our lives, not realizing that there is a purpose. God, in His lovingkindness, will turn attacks of the enemy into fruitful progress for His children. Using the life of Joseph, as well as some courageous companions throughout Scripture, will prove beneficial to us. Within each chapter, we will seek to identify:

- **The Problem**

- **The Lie**

- **The Truth**

- **The Fruit**

> One of the most significant lies we believe is that a temporary situation is a permanent habitation.

Generally speaking, the main problem is not our adversity, but rather our ability to trust in God. One of the most significant lies we believe is that a temporary situation is a permanent habitation. It is essential to realize the truth. Your life isn't over, and God isn't finished. You're just in the middle of your story. There is fruit on the other side of this. Don't give up in the middle.

CHAPTER 2

In the Middle of Comparison

Origins

DENNIS THE MENACE GETS saved! That was what it was like when I made Jesus the Lord and Savior of my life. Most people I knew who found out didn't really believe it. I also didn't shout about it from the rooftops. I don't judge anyone too harshly for being skeptical back then simply because I was wild, crazy, and loud. All my life, I have hit the room before my body does. I have never faded off into the wallpaper. However, I have been working on correcting this for some time now. I want to be in the room without always being the center of attention. Yet, as a teenager, I was unconcerned with such things and stood out intentionally, and unintentionally. Shortly after I returned to school from summer break, my high school counselor called me into her office. Going to the office wasn't a new experience for me. I knew everyone in there and where all the paddles were kept. This was back when corporal punishment was very much all the rage and, in my experience, very effective.

As I slowly and hesitantly approached, I could see that she had a very concerned look on her face. Something was up, and I was racking my brain to figure out what new thing I had done that had landed me back in trouble. She motioned for me to have a seat. She began talking to me, and I immediately noticed she was much more caring than usual. She wanted to know if something terrible had happened to me. She finally pointedly asked if I had been molested or if my parents were divorcing. When I asked what prompted these inquiries, she relayed that most of my teachers had noticed a drastic change in my behavior and were concerned. I laughed out loud. Usually, when the class clown becomes quiet and no longer distracts the class, it is because something terrible has befallen them. In my case, I was acting better because my heart was better. It was clean. I was free. I told her not to worry; Jesus Christ had saved me. She exclaimed, "Hallelujah!" Which may have been a first in that office. She shared that she was also a believer and so glad for me. Needless to say, she was relieved that it wasn't one of the other reasons she had mentioned. This was the first time someone began to see the new person I was becoming in Christ. It would take time before others who knew me could reconcile the old me with this new man. I couldn't blame them.

> I was acting better because
> my heart was better. It was clean.
> I was free. I told her not to worry;
> Jesus Christ had saved me.

Things continued to escalate spiritually for me. About six months later, in 1988, God called me to preach. I was in my room praying while John Starnes sang in the background from my cassette player. I remember it clearly. I had been praying for a couple of hours when I heard God's voice.

In this call, God told me, "Go to all the world and preach the gospel to every creature." Unbeknownst to me at the time, this was a reference to Mark 16:15. In addition to this, He said that I would travel to every continent to share the Gospel. Then, He added something unexpected: I would stand before tens of thousands and even win princes and princesses in the Lord. He showed me that this ministry would be His, and it would be worldwide. People I didn't even know confirmed it in several miraculous ways. Suffice it to say that this call differed from what I had heard from others. Yet, each time it was confirmed, not only did God say that I was called to preach, but it also included the global scope of ministry that He had foretold. I had a vision of it, and it was huge. I was about Joseph's age, and I made Joseph's mistake. I told absolutely EVERYONE. And, in my vanity or at least in my immaturity, I thought God had picked me to be...AWESOME! I had no idea of what would come next.

Joseph's story begins at the end of Genesis 30. It tells of his birth and can easily be passed over when studying his life. However, the seeds of many of his trials are planted before he is even born. To understand Joseph, you must first look at his parents. For those keenly familiar with the Bible, please understand that this book is for everyone.

While many know this story well, I must retell it for those hearing it for the first time.

In Genesis 25, Joseph's father, Jacob, steals his brother Esau's birthright. He coerces Esau into giving up his birthright for a bowl of stew. Later in chapter 27, Jacob impersonates Esau to deceive his blind and ailing father into giving him the firstborn's blessing, which belongs to Esau. Jacob has to flee for his life once Esau discovers his deception. Chapter 29 tells how he meets a beauty named Rachel and works out a deal with her father, Laban. He is to work for seven years to marry her. Laban deceives Jacob and instead gives him Leah, Laban's oldest daughter. Jacob has to agree to work seven more years to marry Rachel. Thus, Jacob becomes the husband of two sisters. It doesn't take great discernment or foresight to guess how having sister wives will turn out. Consider the events preceding Joseph's birth.

Genesis 30 (NASB)

¹ Now when Rachel saw that she bore Jacob no children, she became jealous of her sister; and she said to Jacob, "Give me children, or else I die." ² Then Jacob's anger burned against Rachel, and he said, "Am I in the place of God, who has withheld from you the fruit of the womb?" ³ She said, "Here is my maid Bilhah, go in to her that she may bear on my knees, that through her I too may have children." ⁴ So she gave him her maid Bilhah as a wife, and Jacob went in to her. ⁵ Bilhah conceived and bore Jacob a son. ⁶ Then Rachel said, "God has vindicated me, and has indeed heard my voice and has given me a son." Therefore she named him Dan. [7] Rachel's maid Bilhah conceived again and bore Jacob a second son. [8] So Rachel said, "With mighty wrestlings I have wrestled with my sister, and I have indeed prevailed." And she named him Naphtali. [9] When Leah saw that she had stopped bearing, she took her maid Zilpah and gave her to Jacob as a wife. [10] Leah's maid Zilpah bore Jacob a son. [11] Then Leah said, "How fortunate!" So she named him Gad. [12] Leah's maid Zilpah bore Jacob a second son. [13] Then Leah said, "Happy am I! For women will call me happy." So she named him Asher. [14] Now in the days of wheat harvest Reuben went and found mandrakes in the field and brought them to his mother Leah. Then Rachel said to Leah, "Please give me some of your son's mandrakes." [15] But she said to her, "Is it a small matter for you to take my husband? And would you take my son's mandrakes also?" So Rachel said, "Therefore he may lie with you tonight in return for your son's mandrakes." [16] When Jacob came in from the field in the evening, then Leah went out to meet him and said, "You must come in to me, for I have surely hired you with my son's mandrakes." So he lay with her that night. [17] God gave heed to Leah, and she conceived and bore Jacob a fifth son. [18] Then Leah said, "God has given me my wages because I gave

*my maid to my husband." So she named him
Issachar. [19] Leah conceived again and bore a
sixth son to Jacob. [20] Then Leah said, "God has
endowed me with a good gift; now my husband
will dwell with me, because I have borne
him six sons." So she named him Zebulun. [21]
Afterward she bore a daughter and named her
Dinah. [22] Then God remembered Rachel, and
God gave heed to her and opened her womb. [23]
So she conceived and bore a son and said, "God
has taken away my reproach." [24] She named
him Joseph, saying, "May the Lord give me
another son."*

The Problem: *Comparison and Rivalry*

Rachel and Leah are in fierce competition with each other.
It is a quest for supremacy, or perhaps it is to see who has
more worth. Leah is the first wife, but Rachel is the first
choice. Rachel is beautiful, but Leah is fertile. Rachel finds
a loophole and has two children through her handmaid,
only to spur Leah to do the same. They even have a
financial transaction over who gets to sleep with Jacob one
night.

> Leah is the first wife, but Rachel is the first choice.

This sibling rivalry impacts their children's names. Rachel
calls her first child through her handmaid by the name

of Dan, which means "judge." She believes that God has vindicated her or *judged* her as worthy. The second son is named Naphtali, which means "wrestling." It states in Genesis 30:8 that she names him that because she has wrestled with her sister and prevailed. Leah gets her handmaid to have babies with Jacob and names the first Gad, which means "troop." It is almost like she is trying to amass an army against her sister. And on and on it goes.

This cycle of comparison and the quest for worth continues in an unrighteous fashion until Leah sells some of her son's mandrakes for a night with Jacob. She conceives a baby named Issachar, meaning "there is recompense." She believes God has compensated her for selling the mandrakes for sex. Sexual bartering, competition, manipulation, naming children according to who is winning at the time...wow...it's no wonder that rivalry and comparison become the family business, and what terrible dividends it pays. As bad as all this is, don't forget this toxic environment begins with Jacob.

The Lie: *Your Worth is Found in What You Have to Offer*

We have all experienced the desire to be on top and the nagging sense that we are less than others. We can feel that we don't measure up to someone else, so we compete with them, manipulate them, or perhaps tear them down to raise our status. God promises Jacob the birthright, but he and his mother decide to take matters into their own hands instead of trusting God.

The sibling rivalry between Esau and Jacob set the stage for how Jacob's family will operate. Because Jacob deceives to advance himself, he, in turn, becomes the victim of Laban's deception. He plants the seed that springs up the fruit, Laban's marital switch. The war for supremacy between the sister wives plants the seeds that will bear the fruit of attempted murder, cover-up, and slavery between their children.

> Actions taken out of insecurity, fear, and rivalry never ultimately lead to satisfaction or vindication.

What seeds are you planting that can have terrible consequences for those you haven't met yet? Actions taken out of insecurity, fear, and rivalry never ultimately lead to satisfaction or vindication. They always lead to pain and destruction. Every movie we've ever seen tells this tale. It is one of life's certainties.

Whenever someone feels less than, underappreciated, unworthy, or overlooked, the enemy lies and tries to convince them that humans are the masters of their fate and that they must take matters into their own hands. This is born out of fear and a lack of trust in God's intentions for His children, not to mention that it always ends badly. Leah is compared to Rachel's beauty. Rachel is compared to Leah's fertility. They both war against each other, trying to win their husband's favor and preference.

2 Corinthians 10:12 (NASB)
12 *For we are not bold to class or compare*

ourselves with some of those who commend themselves; but when they measure themselves by themselves and compare themselves with themselves, they are without understanding.

Comparison doesn't lead one to greater understanding but, instead, leaves us without comprehension. The more we look at them...the more we lose sight of self or, more importantly, of Jesus.

So many times, people make the mistake of believing that a better job, bigger house, or more extensive bank account will fix their insecurity. It never does. Whatever we are when we're poor, we are when we're rich. We just have more money to do what we want. You will be even more generous if you were generous before becoming wealthy. But, if you were lustful before you were rich, you will probably spend a lot of money to feed that lust. Acquisition of things doesn't transition your heart's position. For example, cosmetic surgery will not make a woman feel more beautiful or a man more handsome. The clothes may fit the way he or she wants, but if the inside is not addressed, that sense of feeling ugly will remain. That comes from the inside, not the outside.

Comparison doesn't lead one to greater understanding but, instead, leaves us without comprehension.

For all of Rachel's and Leah's children, they only experience more heartache. Leah thinks having eight children will make her the principal wife Jacob will want to live with most of the time. It doesn't. The reason is simple. He loves Rachel more. Rachel thinks having children through her handmaid will fix the internal sense that she isn't good enough. It doesn't. Even when Joseph finally arrives, more trouble is coming because these sisters have taken matters into their own hands. This is a direct result of how Jacob has previously operated with Esau and Isaac. Taking care of business yourself, instead of trusting God to lead your life, tends to bring more costly business your way! Stop trusting your ability to manipulate and trust the One with all authority and power!

The Truth: *Your Worth is Found Only in Him*

When you are in the middle of comparison, don't take the bait and try to end the contest through your own strength. Walk through comparison as a son or daughter of God. What if Jacob were to be generous with Esau the day he returns from the hunt and begs Jacob for some of that red stew? Consider what God has already promised Jacob.

> ### Genesis 25:21-23 (NASB)
> *21 Isaac prayed to the Lord on behalf of his wife, because she was barren; and the Lord answered him and Rebekah his wife conceived. 22 But the children struggled together within her; and she said, "If it is so, why then am I this way?" So she went to inquire of the Lord. 23 The Lord said to her, "Two nations are in your womb; and two peoples will be separated from your body; and*

one people shall be stronger than the other; and the older shall serve the younger."

Before he was even born, God said Jacob would enjoy the position usually reserved for the oldest. What could happen if he were to meet his brother Esau with generosity and compassion? Esau might voluntarily reward him. If Esau were to choose to bestow the birthright on him, he wouldn't be angry with Jacob. It could be given freely instead of coerced. Also, the seeds Jacob plants into his future marriage and children would be entirely different. Instead of competition, comparison, manipulation, and division, a crop could arise in his household that demonstrates cooperation, encouragement, trust, and unity.

Instead of waiting for what we need to be given to us, we often take it. Didn't Jesus say, "Give and it shall be given unto you?" We tend to think we are diminished through the act of giving. That's the world's economy, not God's. What you do now sows seeds into your future and the future of people you haven't met yet! Trusting God brings reward. Trusting yourself brings regret. More than that, when we trust God, He can give us what our strategies and manipulations fail to produce.

We tend to think we are diminished through the act of giving. That's the world's economy, not God's.

The Fruit: *Identity and Purpose*

Ultimately, Rachel doesn't remain barren. She has two children of her own, not to mention the two she has from her handmaiden. Isn't it interesting that we tend to think of this woman with four children as barren? Perhaps it is because that is the way she sees herself. Her perception is that she is barren at the beginning of her marriage, and so she believes it will remain a permanent state. It becomes her identity. The lie is that she is barren for life. The truth is that she is beautiful. The truth is that she is her husband's first love and first choice. The truth is that she won't be barren forever. Rachel doesn't see herself as any of these things, however. She sees herself through the lens of the lie. As stated in the previous chapter, never let temporary circumstances inform your permanent decisions. She believes "RIGHT NOW" is the same as "ALWAYS WILL BE." Once you do that, you can no longer hope that God is moving on your behalf. You believe that you're stuck. This makes your dilemma your idol, and you believe in it more than you do in God's promises. Rachel's belief is so strong that it becomes her identity and even informs how we see her thousands of years later. Isn't that amazing?

Never let temporary circumstances inform your permanent decisions. We must remember that delayed fulfillment gives the glory to God.

In Genesis 15-16, Sarai makes the same error. Because so much time has passed, she trades God's "shall be" for her "may be." She thinks that because it was difficult ten years ago, it's impossible now. Because of her wrong belief, she surrenders the honor of birthing her promise to another! We must remember that delayed fulfillment gives the glory to God. What Rachel essentially does to herself is to establish a finite circumstance as an infinite identity!

What is pressing on you so firmly that you have eschewed faith in God and hope in His promise for the false identity the enemy seeks to assign you? Maybe you have failed recently, but you are not a failure. You may be broke, but you are not poor. People may have left your ministry, but that doesn't mean God is displeased with you. Perhaps your business hasn't panned out like you'd hoped, or your church isn't growing like other churches. These are transient circumstances that don't stay the same forever. Don't allow the enemy to use them as an identity stamper. It's happening to you, but it is *NOT* you. We are more than our circumstances. We are God's children, and He has good things in store for us.

Rachel is destined to become the one who gives Jacob the "son of his old age." This is a place of honor. She lives her life believing she is being left out. That's the lie. That is a misunderstanding of what is actually happening. She isn't being left out; she is being saved for later. As the saying goes, *saving the best for last is often the truth that evades the one being saved for later.*

This divine delay is often excruciating. Just like her husband, Jacob, what would happen if she trusted God?

She could have a wonderful relationship with her sister. She could relieve Jacob's stress. She could be a loving aunt to her nephews. That is a big one. If she were their favorite aunt, who couldn't have children, they would celebrate Joseph's birth and treat him with love instead of contempt. These choices were between fear and love. Kenneth Collins writes of John Wesley in "A Real Christian":

> *Thus, Wesley's seasoned and relatively favorable estimation of the faith of a servant in this sense probably emerged from his consideration that such a faith, in the normal course of spiritual development, would in time become the faith of a child of God. In fact, his sermon "On Faith" (1788), Wesley highlighted just such a consideration: "And, indeed, unless the servants of God halt by the way, they will receive the adoption of sons. They will receive the faith of the children of God by his revealing his only-begotten Son in their hearts...And whosoever hath this, the Spirit of God witnesseth with his spirit that he is a child of God." Likewise, Wesley's appreciation of a degree of acceptance and his exhortation to servants to improve the rich grace of God is revealed in a sermon of 1788, "On the Discoveries of Faith".*
>
> *Whoever has attained this, the faith of a servant...in consequence of which he is in a degree (as the Apostle observes), "accepted with*

him."...Nevertheless he should be exhorted not to stop there; not to rest till he attains the adoption of sons; till he obeys out of love, which is the privilege of all the children of God.Simply put, the faith of a servant of God is valued not only for the measure of faith that it is, but also for what it will soon become: the qualitatively different faith of a child of God, where faith will be filled not with the energy of the fear but with the energy of love.[2]

The whole family dynamic could be altered if Rachel was to choose faith rather than fear. As Wesley points out, if either of these sisters would love without fear, the energies of the children in their household would be driven by love. Our faith must be filled with love, not fear. But we must choose it. We must remember that we aren't making choices that only impact the here and now. We are choosing a path for the future. God has an ordained identity for Rachel. She is the chosen one. He has a purpose for her. She is to give birth to a preserver of life. *A Walk Thru the Life of Joseph* speaks directly about identity and the family's role:

Identity is a complicated thing. Our self-awareness is profoundly shaped by who our family is, by where we come from, and by the work we do, among other factors. So when a person is raised in a dysfunctional family, is removed from his or her own culture, and has to work in a dead-end job, self-identity takes a triple hit. And when those three factors are severely distorted—when the dysfunction involves domestic abuse, the cultural transition is sudden, and the dead-end job is forced labor—well, such trauma could have lasting impact on the person and ripple effects into future generations. Joseph could have checked "all of the above"—a background of abuse, social disadvantages, and hopeless situations—and resigned himself to an obscure, tedious life. Apparently he didn't. He probably couldn't allow himself to. He was driven by a high calling and a firm belief that God was worthy of his obedience and loyalty, regardless of apparent setbacks. If anyone ever had a right to be eaten away by bitterness, Joseph certainly did. Most of his brothers wanted him dead. They settled for sending him away to a distant land in chains. Anything, as long as they didn't have to deal with him. And their venomous attitude toward him resulted in long, painful years as an outsider of extremely low means.[3]

The fruit of pressing through when you are in the middle of comparison is receiving the identity and purpose God intends for you. When you do it God's way, you don't have to settle for the false identity the enemy is trying to assess and assign you.

> The fruit of pressing through when you are in the middle of comparison is receiving the identity and purpose God intends for you.

Psalm 37 sums it up quite nicely.

Psalm 37 (NASB)

1 Do not fret because of evildoers, be not envious toward wrongdoers. 2 For they will wither quickly like the grass and fade like the green herb. 3 Trust in the Lord and do good; dwell in the land and cultivate faithfulness. 4 Delight yourself in the Lord; and He will give you the desires of your heart. 5 Commit your way to the Lord, trust also in Him, and He will do it. 6 He will bring forth your righteousness as the light and your judgment as the noonday. 7 Rest in the Lord and wait patiently for Him; do not fret because of him who prospers in his way, because of the man who carries out wicked schemes. 8 Cease from anger and forsake wrath; do not fret; it leads only to evildoing. 9 For evildoers will be cut off, but those who wait for the Lord, they will inherit the land. 10 Yet a little while and the wicked man will be no more; and you will look carefully for his place and he will not be there. 11 But the humble will inherit the land and will delight themselves in abundant prosperity. 12 The wicked plots against the

righteous and gnashes at him with his teeth.
[13] The Lord laughs at him, for He sees his
day is coming. [14] The wicked have drawn
the sword and bent their bow to cast down
the afflicted and the needy, to slay those who
are upright in conduct. [15] Their sword will
enter their own heart, and their bows will be
broken. [16] Better is the little of the righteous
than the abundance of many wicked. [17] For
the arms of the wicked will be broken, but
the Lord sustains the righteous. [18] The Lord
knows the days of the blameless, and their
inheritance will be forever. [19] They will not
be ashamed in the time of evil, and in the
days of famine they will have abundance. [20]
But the wicked will perish; and the enemies of
the Lord will be like the glory of the pastures,
they vanish—like smoke they vanish away. [21]
The wicked borrows and does not pay back,
but the righteous is gracious and gives. [22] For
those blessed by Him will inherit the land, but
those cursed by Him will be cut off. [23] The
steps of a man are established by the Lord,
and He delights in his way. [24] When he falls,
he will not be hurled headlong, because the
Lord is the One who holds his hand. [25] I have
been young and now I am old, yet I have not
seen the righteous forsaken or his descendants
begging bread. [26] All day long he is gracious
and lends, and his descendants are a blessing.
[27] Depart from evil and do good, so you will

abide forever. [28] For the Lord loves justice and does not forsake His godly ones; they are preserved forever, but the descendants of the wicked will be cut off. [29] The righteous will inherit the land and dwell in it forever. [30] The mouth of the righteous utters wisdom, and his tongue speaks justice. [31] The law of his God is in his heart; his steps do not slip. [32] The wicked spies upon the righteous and seeks to kill him. [33] The Lord will not leave him in his hand or let him be condemned when he is judged. [34] Wait for the Lord and keep His way, and He will exalt you to inherit the land; when the wicked are cut off, you will see it. [35] I have seen a wicked, violent man spreading himself like a luxuriant tree in its native soil. [36] Then he passed away, and lo, he was no more; I sought for him, but he could not be found. [37] Mark the blameless man, and behold the upright; for the man of peace will have a posterity. [38] But transgressors will be altogether destroyed; the posterity of the wicked will be cut off. [39] But the salvation of the righteous is from the Lord; He is their strength in time of trouble. [40] The Lord helps them and delivers them; He delivers them from the wicked and saves them, because they take refuge in Him.

CHAPTER 3

In the Middle of Rejection

There Is No Guarantee of Acceptance

No matter how smart or accomplished you are, you cannot guarantee acceptance by others.

THERE ARE FEW, IF any, who have not felt rejected. Its sting is painful and, many times, long-lasting. In some cases, it is life-altering. What do you do when you're rejected? Many handle it in very dysfunctional ways. A person who feels rejected may build walls up to isolate themselves and preemptively keep themselves from being rejected again. This may stave off *new* rejection, but it can lock the person into the fallout of the last rejection. In other words, they continue in a perpetual state of hurt and bitterness, which keeps the rejection alive and well. It's like wanting not to get bitten by any more lions, so you lock yourself in the cage with the last lion who bit you! You're now safe from any *other* lions but still at the mercy of the one that made you afraid in the first place.

Still others dive headfirst into performance, religion, and perfectionism. They seem to have adopted the belief that if they run faster and jump higher, they will be accepted. More success, money, power, and the like are sought after to be good enough to merit the acceptance of others. This is an orphan mentality. Unlike sons and daughters who trust the Father to protect them and provide all their needs, the orphan mindset seeks to protect and provide for itself. No matter how smart or accomplished you are, you cannot guarantee acceptance by others. The reason is simple. Jealousy and rejection are kinsmen. A common reaction to jealousy is to reject the object of one's envy. When this occurs, the rejection is born of something you are or have that the other person desires. Performing better isn't the cure. It would actually cause more jealousy! If you are caught in the middle of this vicious cycle, you are not alone. Joseph experienced it as well.

The Problem: *Jealousy and Rejection*

Genesis 37:1-11 (NASB)
¹Now Jacob lived in the land where his father had sojourned, in the land of Canaan. ² These are the records of the generations of Jacob. Joseph, when seventeen years of age, was pasturing the flock with his brothers while he was still a youth, along with the sons of Bilhah

and the sons of Zilpah, his father's wives. And Joseph brought back a bad report about them to their father. ³ **Now Israel loved Joseph more than all his sons, because he was the son of his old age; and he made him a varicolored tunic.** ⁴ **His brothers saw that their father loved him more than all his brothers; and so they hated him and could not speak to him on friendly terms.** ⁵ **Then Joseph had a dream, and when he told it to his brothers, they hated him even more.** ⁶ *He said to them, "Please listen to this dream which I have had;* ⁷ *for behold, we were binding sheaves in the field, and lo, my sheaf rose up and also stood erect; and behold, your sheaves gathered around and bowed down to my sheaf."* ⁸ *Then his brothers said to him, "Are you actually going to reign over us? Or are you really going to rule over us?"* **So they hated him even more for his dreams and for his words.** ⁹ *Now he had still another dream, and related it to his brothers, and said, "Lo, I have had still another dream; and behold, the sun and the moon and eleven stars were bowing down to me."* ¹⁰ *He related it to his father and to his brothers; and* **his father rebuked him** *and said to him, "What is this dream that you have had? Shall I and your mother and your brothers actually come to bow ourselves down before you to the ground?"* ¹¹ **His brothers**

were jealous of him, but his father kept the saying in mind *(emphasis added).*

Joseph is born into a family devoted to sibling rivalry and competition. The mothers are in a battle for who will dominate the other. Leah even named her last baby Zebulun, meaning "exalted," because she thought her many sons would exalt her above her sister in receiving affection from their husband, Jacob. They have sown seeds of jealousy and rejection. The sons continue this process.

After Joseph is born, Jacob, who himself has also sown seeds of deception and passed this dysfunctional behavior on to his sons, is overjoyed to not only have a biological son with Rachel but one in his old age. Consequently, he celebrates him. He does so by favoring Joseph and giving him pricey gifts. None of these outside forces are Joseph's fault. But it makes him the target of his brothers' jealousy. Jacob gives Joseph an expensive coat of many colors which only adds fuel to the fire. Now, he is dressed in a manner that identifies him as unique and favored. It's like wearing a bullseye.

Then something else happens. He receives a dream from God that seems to indicate his future dominion over his brothers. He shares it with his brothers for reasons passing understanding, and they hate him even more. Some fault Joseph for provoking his brothers by rubbing their noses in it. Others hold to the idea that he was naïve and, therefore, innocent. *A Walk Thru the Life of Joseph* puts it this way:

*In favor of "innocent/righteous/naïve" is the
fact that the Bible never speaks a negative
word about Joseph. He's one of only a
handful of others whose flaws are not directly
mentioned. (Ruth, Esther, and Daniel—in
addition to the most obvious case, Jesus—are
most prominent among those select few.) The
messianic symbolism in Joseph's experiences
also supports the idea of his innocence, and
the ensuing behavior of his brothers proves
that they likely would have been bothered by
a righteous son in their midst regardless of
whether he flaunted it or not. On the other
hand, what does it say of the character of
a seventeen-year-old that he tattles, displays
his status symbol prominently, and blatantly
defies social norms by expressing his visions
of grandeur to older men in the family? After
all, in a highly paternalistic culture in which
fathers are the highest authority and sons are
ranked by seniority, you don't just tell eleven
men who are higher in the pecking order that
they'll bow before you. And, in fact, Joseph's
family may think he expects the dreams to have
immediate implications—as in, "you should
bow to me now."*[4]

I can only say from my own experience that the
promise and favor of the father are exciting, especially
as a teenager. Sharing that promise without considering
how others might receive the revelation or how they

perceive you can prove to stir up turmoil. I made the same mistake as Joseph, and whether it was intentional or not, the effect was terrible and immediate. From his brothers' perspective, the dream not only indicates Joseph is their father's favorite, but he is God's favorite as well.

Joseph has another dream indicating that he will also rule over his parents. The brothers hate Jacob's affection toward Joseph, his special coat, and his dreams. They, too, want to be loved, regarded, and favored. They have likely been trained to fight for affection and attention through witnessing years of rivalry between their mothers. This is the heart of their rejection. Joseph's brothers want their father's love and approval. They aren't rejecting Joseph as much as they are rejecting their father's favoritism.

> They aren't rejecting Joseph as much as they are rejecting the father's favoritism.

Jacob's overwhelming neglect of celebrating his other sons in light of his jubilant celebration of Joseph brought contempt, bitterness, and hurt. Imagine having worked for years to earn favor and promotion only to be overlooked for a younger brother who has not invested his life into building the family business or raising up heirs. Jacob's acceptance and exaltation of Joseph feels like a rejection of the other sons' identity and merit. This creates a highly toxic and competitive family dynamic where the sons think they can't address the matter with Jacob and instead project their anger and pain onto Joseph.

Remember, when rejection comes, while it feels intensely personal, it may not be about us. Most of the time, it is about that empty place inside of the ones doing the rejecting. My wife and I have a couple that mentors us. He and my wife react similarly to rejection, while His wife and I respond differently. Whenever someone does one of us wrong...he and my precious wife ask, "I wonder what's wrong with me?" His wife and I ask, "I wonder what's wrong with them?!" Usually, people react out of pain or for some other reason. If you can keep that in mind, it may help mitigate the flood of negative emotions that come with being treated poorly.

And, of course, it should be noted that Joseph doesn't help himself by telling his brothers, who are already against him, what God has shown him. He probably does this because he knows who he is now more than ever. After all, God has shown him the end of his story. Besides, the dream seems to communicate a nearing present reality, with sheaves bowing down to him as they all work in their father's fields. It likely doesn't occur to Joseph how far out the vision is from coming to pass.

Have you ever had a dream or vision from God? He shows you the future, and it colors everything from then on. God's Word should renew your mind so that you don't feel like competing with others or worrying about what they think of you. His Word and the dreams He gives us empower us to change our thinking and how we live our lives.

> *He cannot express any more in us than what we*
> *concluded we are in Him. So, if we do not know who*
> *we are in Him first, He will be unable to fully express*
> *what he desires in us.*

Consider Robert Smith's words in *Elimination of Erroneous Distinctions*:[5]

> *If a person does not yet have an understanding*
> *of God's Word, he is not renewed in his*
> *mind. Therefore, he is still laboring under*
> *the old fleshly syndrome of self-preservation.*
> *The doctrine of self-preservation supports the*
> *notion that you can save yourself and that you*
> *must do for yourself if you want to be accepted*
> *by God. Thankfully, the Christian journey*
> *does not start there. To the contrary, we start*
> *from a position of total dependency, with the*
> *knowledge that God is the only one who can*
> *save us. After receiving the Lord Jesus Christ as*
> *our personal savior, we must get into the word*
> *of God and be swift to discover what it means.*
> *We must forget about what we were and begin*
> *to think about who we are: We are accepted in*
> *Him. We are completed in Him. We are buried*
> *with Him. We are raised with Him. We are*
> *seated with Him. We start our journey having*
> *all these benefits. The progression reveals who*
> *he is in us. He cannot express any more in us*
> *than what we concluded we are in Him. So, if*

we do not know who we are in Him first, He
will be unable to fully express what he desires
in us.

Think of that! You start from the end, like when David, as a boy, is anointed King. The realization of that in the government doesn't happen for quite some time, but in the spirit, he is King from his youth. Who does God say you are? What has He promised you? You don't have to wait to walk in that identity. You can live it now in the spirit.

The Lie: *You Aren't Chosen*

For the person enduring rejection, it can be difficult to realize that things are not as they seem. Rejection seems to say, "You aren't enough. You're not good enough. You're not chosen." However, in Joseph's case, the rejection is because of his brothers' jealousy. They feel that they are not enough for their father and hate Joseph because he is. It's an illusion. It seems one way but is actually another. How often have you seen a child be mean to another child, making them feel like they don't belong, or something is wrong with them? Yet, later, you discover that the child was envious of how the other one looked or what they had. The one being exclusive and hateful was feeling like they didn't measure up and acted out.

If anyone ever endured rejection, it was Jesus. Many occasions are written about in the Bible where He is rejected for various reasons. Mark 6 and Matthew 13 recount how He came to Nazareth, but the people couldn't receive Him because they knew Him growing up.

Mark 6:1-6 (NASB)

[1] Jesus went out from there and came into His hometown; and His disciples followed Him. [2] When the Sabbath came, He began to teach in the synagogue; and the many listeners were astonished, saying, "Where did this man get these things, and what is this wisdom given to Him, and such miracles as these performed by His hands? [3] **Is not this the carpenter, the son of Mary, and brother of James and Joses and Judas and Simon? Are not His sisters here with us***?" And they took offense at Him. [4] Jesus said to them,* **"A prophet is not without honor except in his hometown** *and among his own relatives and in his own household." [5] And He could do no miracle there except that He laid His hands on a few sick people and healed them. [6] And He wondered at their unbelief (emphasis added).*

This Scripture became especially important to me when I went back to my hometown to pastor. While I knew of this Scripture, I never really noticed that many Bibles print it in red ink! And I can tell you that Jesus was serious about this. His words still ring true today. More on that later. Suffice to say, many cities repent due to Jesus' teaching, but the Galilean towns of Chorazin, Bethsaida, Capernaum, and Decapolis refuse to repent. In response, Jesus declares the wicked cities of Tyre, Sidon, Sodom, and Gomorrah would have repented, and it would be more bearable for them on Judgement Day than for the cities rejecting Him (Matthew 11:23, Luke 10:13-15). Additionally, in Luke 9, Jesus is not welcomed in Samaria because He is headed to Jerusalem. Scripture reveals the ethnic hatred between Jews and Samaritans.

There is one significant account. In John 6, Jesus is telling the sizeable crowd that unless they eat His flesh and drink His blood, they can have no part with Him. Of course, He is speaking of communion in a spiritual sense, but most cannot discern it. Instead, they respond with disgust and leave Him.

John 6:56-71 (NASB)

[56] *"He who eats My flesh and drinks My blood abides in Me, and I in him.* [57] *As the living Father sent Me, and I live because of the Father, so he who eats Me, he also will live because of Me.* [58] *This is the bread which came down out of heaven; not as the fathers ate and died; he who eats this bread will live forever."* [59] *These things He said in the synagogue as He taught in Capernaum.* [60] *Therefore many of His disciples, when they heard this said,* **"This is a difficult statement; who can listen to it?"** [61] *But Jesus, conscious that His disciples grumbled at this, said to them, "Does this cause you to stumble?* [62] *What then if you see the Son of Man ascending to where He was before?* [63] *It is the Spirit who gives life; the flesh profits nothing; the words that I have spoken to you are spirit and are life.* [64] *But there are some*

of you who do not believe." For Jesus knew from the beginning who they were who did not believe, and who it was that would betray Him. ⁶⁵ And He was saying, "For this reason I have said to you, that no one can come to Me unless it has been granted him from the Father." **⁶⁶ As a result of this many of His disciples withdrew and were not walking with Him anymore.** *⁶⁷ So Jesus said to the twelve,* **"You do not want to go away also, do you?"** *⁶⁸ Simon Peter answered Him, "Lord, to whom shall we go? You have words of eternal life. ⁶⁹ We have believed and have come to know that You are the Holy One of God." ⁷⁰ Jesus answered them, "Did I Myself not choose you, the twelve, and yet one of you is a devil?" ⁷¹ Now He meant Judas the son of Simon Iscariot, for he, one of the twelve, was going to betray Him (emphasis added).*

Be free of performance right now! Jesus is perfect in every way. He is flawless in word and deed, yet His ministry would not be considered a success by today's standards. Numerically, it wouldn't measure up. Even when the crowds were large, Jesus drove supposed followers away by His speech. His rhetoric is divisive, and He doesn't seem to be able to play to the tender sensibilities of His audience. Here is a prime example. They all leave Him except the twelve; even one of them is plotting betrayal. Jesus turns to them, no doubt discouraged and asks if they also want to leave Him. What a moment!

> Perfectionism and performance don't keep you from
> being rejected. Don't believe the lie.

Do you think that you can outperform Jesus? Can you *do* ministry better than Him? Can you be a better preacher than Him? Can you pray more, hear more clearly from the Father, or live more perfectly than Him? Of course not! Despite His perfection, ability to perform great signs and wonders, and never-ending love – in the end, He faces Pilate alone, He faces the religious Pharisees by Himself, and He carries His cross to Golgotha. Perfectionism and performance don't keep you from being rejected. Don't believe the lie.

The Truth: *You've Been Chosen by the Father*

Joseph is not rejected because he is less than his brothers but because his father accepts him. Jesus also endures immense rejection because of His relationship with the Heavenly Father. When you face rejection, you must ask yourself, "What are they rejecting?" If you can clarify the object of their rejection, you won't spin your wheels fixing the wrong problem. Too many times, we don't ask the Holy Spirit for help. *We make decisions instead of getting instructions. We assume instead of interceding.* This will usually shoot us off on a wild goose chase. Next time, ask the Holy Spirit, "What are they rejecting?" You will probably be shocked by the answer. Most of the time, the answer will be, "Me." That's right...God in you. This is why most people reject believers. The light in a believer is offensive to the darkness in an unbeliever. Your spirit pesters their demons!

> If you are a herald of truth, those who want to walk in darkness will not hang out with you or stay in your ministry.

As a pastor or minister, when people move away from you; instead of assuming that it's because of a deficit in you or receiving their blame, ask God why they are leaving. Time after time, you will discover that most people leave because they want to sin. If you are a herald of truth, those who want to walk in darkness will not hang out with you or stay in your ministry. They want to go where they can do what they want without accountability.

The crowds following Jesus reject communion with Him. Like the Pharisees later demonstrate themselves, the crowds are intimidated by Jesus' authority and power. When we reflect Jesus, we can count on it being offensive to those hiding from Him. Rest in knowing that you're in good company. Only one disciple is present at Jesus' crucifixion! Everyone else leaves Him. His closest disciples LEAVE HIM! Don't derive your worth from the crowd or others, which God can only establish and keep. If you do, you'll always be chasing the wrong thing.

The Fruit: *The Father*

John 15:18-25 (NASB)

[18] "If the world hates you, you know that it has hated Me before it hated you. [19] If you were of the world, the world would love its own; but because you are not of the world, but I chose you out of the world, because of this the world hates you. [20] Remember the word that I said to you, 'A slave is not greater than his master.' If they persecuted Me, they will also persecute you; if they kept My word, they will keep yours also. [21] But all these things they will do to you for My name's sake, because they do not know the One who sent Me. [22] If I had not come and spoken to them, they would not have sin, but now they have no excuse for their sin. [23] He who hates Me hates My Father also. [24] If I had not done among them the works which no one else did, they would not have sin; but now they have both seen and hated Me and My Father as well. [25] But they have done this to fulfill the word that is written in their Law, 'They hated Me without a cause.'"

As stated earlier, the real desire of Joseph's brothers isn't to see him suffer. They want what Joseph has: the love and favor of their father, Jacob. Jesus lays it out plainly. If the world hated Him, they will hate you. If they persecuted Him, they will persecute you. The world rejects God and His Son. Why are you surprised when you, too, are rejected? This is the dynamic of humankind – it's part of being a family. And what the world doesn't understand is that, unlike Jacob, God desires to pour out His love and favor on anyone who would receive Him. He has a garment of favor awaiting each of us. The issue is whether or not we choose to identify as sons and daughters through faith in Jesus and obey the Father's Word. John 1:11 reads, "He came to His own, and those who were His own did not receive Him."

I began to minister as a teenager in high school. However, I wasn't allowed to speak on a Sunday. "You can preach on Wednesday night," the pastor of my home church finally told me. Back then, Wednesday night services were the minor leagues of the church world. This is where all the singers and preachers who weren't quite ready for the big show (Sunday morning) were sent to. I was viewed as a *Single-A* wannabe preacher and, of course, some thought I still needed to get saved. I did ok, I guess. I preached on Wednesday evenings for a while, then graduated to a tag team preaching with a few others. I would tag team preach with the pastor and a friend of mine who was greener than I was at preaching. We preached on an assigned passage of Scripture. My friend would start (probably because the crowd was most sympathetic at the beginning), I would go next, and the pastor would bat clean up (to round out the baseball metaphor). That way, he could correct anything we had messed up. The exciting thing was that it was on a Sunday. It was Sunday night, but still, it wasn't Wednesday. We were playing *Double-A* ball now! It went well, and we did it several times. But still, no call came from the Majors. I was still Dennis the Menace to many. I wondered if I would ever get a shot.

I know I am writing this in a semi-humorous manner. That is entirely intentional. Let me just put your mind at ease. I didn't view what I was doing as a sport or take it lightly. But I knew I wasn't trusted or at least deemed ready for *prime time*, as they say. Then something happened. I was praying and asking the Lord about this. I knew the pastor couldn't always give up his pulpit, but I really wanted to preach and didn't know how to make that happen. I asked God to help me. He did. But it was in a very unexpected way.

The City-Wide Male Chorus came to sing at our church. They were all African American men from different ethnic churches in our city, which was something I had never experienced before. They were all dressed in suits and looking sharp. Young and old, they sang in a way that immediately captivated me. I had grown up with a lot of Southern Gospel music. My mom and her sisters had a Southern Gospel group and traveled around Texas. For several years, I was their soundman. I didn't care for Southern Gospel as a kid, although now it seems to play constantly on the soundtrack of my mind. The music always seemed to be about heaven, leaving this sad, stinking world behind. As a red-blooded male teenager, I wasn't thinking of heaven's streets of gold...I just wanted to kiss a girl! I wasn't quite ready to see Jesus! Anyways, along came the City-Wide Male Chorus, which had very different music. I loved it immediately.

After they finished, several more groups and individuals sang because this was a worship night event. Then it was my turn. I don't remember what I sang, but something in me connected to them, as I would later find out. After service, several of these men asked me about coming to their church to sing. I hadn't realized that several of these men were pastors. I heartily accepted. For a time, I was regularly singing in these churches. As relationships were built, I said, "I love to sing, but I sure wish I could also preach". One pastor asked, "You preach?" To which I sheepishly replied, "Yes?" I wasn't much of a preacher yet, but he immediately told me he'd gladly let me preach at his church the following Sunday. I finally got my shot, but it was in a different league, and this freckled-faced, reddish-brown-haired boy didn't know all the rules.

I began to preach at these churches; so, in a way, I started my ministry in predominantly African American black churches. While I hadn't grown up with their traditions, I learned quickly. Not only that, but it was also like I had found my people. What I mean is this. They encouraged preaching with passion, emotion, humor, and depth. I was able to be myself. My style was greatly influenced by those precious few years I spent preaching in these churches that welcomed me with open arms. It didn't matter to them what color I was. Because I loved Jesus...I was welcome. I thank God for them. I loved those years and think of them often. They helped me see there was a different way...not everything is one size fits all.

I felt a liberty to be bold, authoritative, Pentecostal, and funny...all at the same time.

I was terribly uncomfortable with some of the norms being thrust upon me by my own faith tradition. It was like a square peg being hammered into a round hole. You had to be serious throughout your presentation and say "HA!" at the end of each sentence. I was certainly demonstrative and Pentecostal in style, but I was also funny. I think I could have been a stand-up comedian. In these churches, I could embrace my humorous side. I know there is humor in preaching, but the occasional laugh isn't what I'm talking about. Imagine Robin Williams getting saved, and you are closer to my storytelling style. I felt a liberty to be bold, authoritative, Pentecostal, and funny...all at the same time. I am so grateful for them.

After a while, I was invited to preach on a Sunday at my home church, and it went pretty well. This continued, and after graduating high school, I began evangelizing. I stood in the back of the state campground auditorium dressed in a suit, trying to meet pastors and ask them if I could preach at their church. It was a statewide meeting that happened once a year, and I received zero invitations. Most of them knew me from my youth camp days and wanted nothing to do with "that crazy kid." I had a suit up to my eyeballs, a calendar in my breast pocket, and newly printed cards with my name, number, and favorite Scripture on them. But alas, no one picked me. I felt rejected and dejected.

He said, "Promotion doesn't come from the North or the South, the East or the West. Promotion only comes from the Father above."

Finally, one pastor came up to me. I was excited, hoping I was about to get my first booking. He told me that God wanted him to tell me something. He said, "Promotion doesn't come from the North or the South, the East or the West. Promotion only comes from the Father above." He turned around and walked off. I was stunned. I was...irritated. Then...I was sorrowful. I know I was wild and crazy and the author of some legendary pranks at youth camp, but I had been transformed. Why couldn't anyone see that? After all, I had a sharp suit on! I turned around to the wall and began to cry. Bubbling up from my rejection, a prayer made its way from my heart, through my lips, and up to heaven. "God, never again will I pursue self-advancement. I will only go where you send me. I will be faithful to whatever you give me to do, and I won't seek promotion. I will seek to be obedient to your direction. I am done trying to make it happen in ministry. I will go where you send me and where you don't...I won't go." I will never forget that moment.

The next day was a morning service that was primarily attended by pastors. I came to the service in a T-shirt, jeans, and a pair of high-tops. It was the early 90's, and that just wasn't the acceptable dress in those days. In the middle of the worship, someone began to speak in tongues. Everything stopped, and the people listened and then waited for the interpretation. This is accepted in Pentecostal and charismatic circles and is laid out for the church in 1 Corinthians 14.

I believed the Lord had given me the interpretation, and even though I felt conspicuous in my attire amid the sea of suits, God had chosen me to deliver His message to that body. It was like a bomb hit that place in the spirit. There was an eruption, and many pastors began flooding the altars. I also went forward and was thankful for what God had done in us.

Afterward, as I was leaving, a dozen pastors gathered around me in the lobby and began telling me of the interpretation's impact on them. One seasoned and respected pastor said where everyone could hear, "Son, if I ever heard God...I heard Him today. I want to book you for a revival." Immediately, many others began to invite me to preach at their churches. I couldn't wrap my brain around it.

> I could just be who He made me to be and go where He sent me. He had chosen me, and He was enough.

Sometime later, as I reflected on that scene in the lobby, I realized the truth about what God had said to me. Promotion comes only from above. I felt rejected in my home church, denomination, and in general. But God's promises are "Yes and amen". I didn't need to make myself something I wasn't. I didn't need to dress up in Saul's armor. I could just be who He made me to be and go where He sent me. He had chosen me, and He was enough.

The truth is that all the bookings came because of absolutely NOTHING I did. It was His interpretation that impacted them. It was His words they responded to. It was His power that changed them at the altar. The only thing

I had done was to say "Yes" to Him. Never forget that an obedient "Yes" to the Lord always opens doors.

> The fruit of pressing through rejection is that you get the Father.

Don't believe the lie that you aren't chosen because you've been rejected. Embrace the truth that you have been chosen already, which is why you face rejection. The fruit of pressing through rejection is that you get the Father. If you chase the approval of men, you will only have the chase because the approval of men is rare and fleeting. But, if you press through, you will get the Father, not just His approval. He is your reward! When facing rejection, ask yourself: "IS *HE* ENOUGH FOR ME?" Isn't that the struggle with rejection? We believe that what was taken from us is more significant than God. And that He isn't enough.

Joseph's story crystallizes the temptation of rejection: "What should have been at the hands of others is greater than what can be at the hand of God." Over time, rejection removes the names and says, "What should have been, is greater than what can be." And God gets unwittingly pushed to the side. Instead, reject the lie of rejection and choose the fruit of the truth...don't worry about the people who didn't pick you...pick God.

CHAPTER 4

In the Middle of Betrayal

Genesis 37:18-36 (NASB)

18 When they saw him from a distance and before he came close to them, they plotted against him to put him to death. 19 They said to one another, **"Here comes this dreamer! 20 Now then, come and let us kill him and throw him into one of the pits; and we will say, 'A wild beast devoured him.' Then let us see what will become of his dreams!"** *21 But Reuben heard this and rescued him out of their hands and said, "Let us not take his life." 22 Reuben further said to them, "Shed no blood. Throw him into this pit that is in the wilderness, but do not lay hands on him"—that he might rescue him out of their hands, to restore him to his father. 23 So it came about, when Joseph reached his brothers, that* **they stripped Joseph of his tunic,** *the varicolored* *tunic that was on him;* ²⁴ *and they took him and threw him into the pit. Now the pit was empty, without any water in it.* ²⁵ *Then they sat down to eat a meal. And as they raised their eyes and looked, behold, a caravan of Ishmaelites was coming from Gilead, with their camels bearing aromatic gum and balm and myrrh, on their way to bring them down to Egypt.* ²⁶ ***Judah said to his brothers, "What profit is it for us to kill our brother and cover up his blood?*** ²⁷ ***Come and let us sell him to the Ishmaelites and not lay our hands on him, for he is our brother, our own flesh****." And his brothers listened to him.* ²⁸ *Then some Midianite traders passed by, so they pulled him up and lifted Joseph out of the pit, and sold him to the Ishmaelites for twenty shekels of silver. Thus they brought Joseph into Egypt.* ²⁹ *Now Reuben returned to the pit, and behold, Joseph was not in the pit; so he tore his garments.* ³⁰ *He returned to his brothers and said, "The boy is not there; as for me, where am I to go?"* ³¹ *So they took Joseph's tunic, and slaughtered a male goat and dipped the tunic in the blood;* ³² *and they sent the varicolored tunic and brought it to their father and said, "We found this; please examine it to see whether it is your son's tunic or not."* ³³ *Then he examined it and said, "It is my son's tunic. A wild beast has devoured him; Joseph has surely been torn to pieces!"* ³⁴ ***So Jacob*** *tore his clothes, and put sackcloth on his loins and mourned for his son many days. ³⁵ Then all his sons and all his daughters arose to comfort him, but he refused to be comforted. And he said, "Surely I will go down to Sheol in mourning for my son." So his father wept for him.* ³⁶ Meanwhile, the Midianites sold him in Egypt to Potiphar, Pharaoh's officer, the captain of the bodyguard (emphasis added).

The Problem: *Betrayal and Loss*

The fruit of all the rivalry, jealousy, competition, deception, and rejection for two generations is a plot among brothers to kill their younger brother. It is altered a bit, and they settle for faking his death and selling him into slavery. Even if they hadn't first set out to murder him, this second scenario is evil enough. Only in the light of what is really in their heart does the latter plan come as a relief. This is important to remember. The enemy is trying to build something. He is patiently constructing a device to steal, kill, and destroy not just you but your family and, ultimately, the dream or purposes of God for your family.

I was a volunteer youth director at my home church for a year; then, I began to evangelize for a couple of years. This was a whole new thing, and it seemed to get better and better. The more I went to other churches, cities, and people groups, the more I grew as a minister. Much of what it takes to be effective in ministry can only come from experience. I relished it. I thought that I would do it for the rest of my life.

After a year, I was finally booked up a year in advance. I moved out on my own and thought that things would get rolling. I couldn't wait to get this worldwide ministry started. Just then...God ruined everything. He told me suddenly, without warning, to cancel everything and attend college. I was floored. Why? To learn how to do what I was already doing? This made no sense to me. It's much too long of a story to convey here but suffice it to say that God's initial direction was miraculously confirmed once again. Within twenty-four hours, I had left Texas and moved to Tennessee.

The first day I was on campus...THE FIRST DAY...I met Rhea, who, unbeknownst to me then, would become the love of my life and the mother of my children. She rode in my car; we went to the movies; we immediately knew...we *didn't* like each other...for a couple of years! But that's not the point of this. College was amazing. I learned more than I thought possible; joined a choir (Rhea was also in it) that was like being in full-time ministry; was mentored by a man who revolutionized my life; and, most importantly...I won the heart of sweet, beautiful, astounding Rhea. Everything I did seemed to do well.

Then we got married and moved to Florida. We worked at her dad's church and school. The school grew; Disney hired Rhea's choirs and ensembles; we had a fist full of Disney World tickets; and the youth group grew and grew. It was a vibrant time, and everything we did seemed to do well.

God called us back to Tennessee four years later to get our master's degrees. We also wound up working at a church in Tennessee. It was Camelot. The youth group exploded. Everything was awesome. Rhea was leading worship, and it was awesome. We built a house, and it was awesome. We had two kids, and they were awesome. We were awesome. Everything we touched seemed to turn to gold. At least, that's how we felt.

Then God ruined it all again. He called me to plant a church in my hometown. That's where the awesomeness evaporated. I had received the dream from God long ago and, in my vain imagination, pictured myself as the head of a great ministry. In my mind, I compared it to other well-known ministries of the day. I just knew it would be bigger, better, and more awesome. I was laying the foundation in my heart for quite the heartbreak.

Remember, when we compare ourselves by ourselves, we're without knowledge. I guess that made me clueless. I had no idea how to interpret the vision God had given me and made the mistake of equating my interpretation with His intention. *Read that again.*

I had no idea how to interpret the vision God had given me and made the mistake of equating my interpretation with His intention.

Jesus said that a prophet is not without honor except in his hometown. As I noted previously, those words are in red! Why would He call me to go to my hometown and be without honor? It felt like a giant step backward.

I would see the truth of Jesus' statement up close and personal. It was problematic from the beginning. Rhea and I experienced more hurt, blame, and betrayal in the first year of our ministry there than we ever had. And the first year was only the beginning. Family members turned on us. Friends, people on our team, church members, and the list goes on of those who would tell us how much we meant to them and what a difference we made in their lives, only to be discarded by them later.

Bondage is always the goal of comparison.

It was like God had dropped us off in the wilderness to die. The toll it took on my wife and even my children was excruciating. I'd look at other friends of mine. I'd see what God was doing in their ministry and compare. I didn't need anyone to compare me to others...I did that all by myself, and it was miserable. I could feel the enemy trying to put shackles on us. Bondage is always the goal of comparison. God brought me here for a reason, but the enemy wanted to use it as an opportunity to destroy us. I had a choice to make.

The choices we make dictate whether or not the enemy is successful in finishing his attack with his weapon of mass destruction. When we give in to comparison, it leads to rejection, which gives birth to betrayal. Betrayal seeks to bind. As I said earlier, bondage is its goal, and the devastation is vast. Again, look at Joseph. Not only is he literally bound up as a slave, but his father is bound up in grief, and the brothers are bound up in guilt. When betrayal wins, everyone is left in chains.

The Lie: *You Can't Trust Anyone*

To the one who is betrayed, the enemy tries to convince them that they can never trust anyone again. This is a ploy to isolate those who are hurt. The reason is very simple. It's all about hunting. **1 Peter 5:8 (NASB)** reads, "Be of sober spirit, be on the alert. Your adversary, the devil, prowls around like a roaring lion, seeking someone to devour." The devil hunts like a lion, and they prefer to go after the prey that are isolated. They don't attack the herd. If you receive the lie that you can't trust anyone and lock yourself away from everyone, then the enemy can more easily attack you in your isolation.

Consider the incredible story of Hosea and Gomer. In the Old Testament book of Hosea, we find that God has Hosea marry a prostitute as a prophetic act representing God being married to Israel even though they have gone astray to other gods. He provides for her needs; gives her a home; has children with her; and even loves her. Gomer is redeemed in every way Hosea could offer. Yet, she betrays his love and goes back to prostitution. Not only is it a massive act of faith and obedience to marry a prostitute at God's command, but then to be rewarded with betrayal has to seem overwhelming. He has loved her, and she rewards him with adultery. After this, her life begins to unravel, and her condition gets so bad that she finds herself being sold as a slave.

> It is unnatural to meet betrayal with trust and
> obedience. It's supernatural!

How do you handle betrayal? Do you lash out in revenge, isolate yourself in an anti-trust bubble, or give yourself over to manipulation and control? Has any of those reactions helped? What if you instead responded by heading deeper into obedience? It is unnatural to meet betrayal with trust and obedience. Actually, it's more than unnatural. It's supernatural! The carnal ways we deal with betrayal do not help us. But trusting God will. It is the only way to get through it. Look what God asks of Hosea after she betrays him.

> **Hosea 3:1-2 (NASB)**
> *[1] Then the Lord said to me,* **"Go <u>again</u>, love a woman who is loved by her husband, yet an adulteress, even as the Lord loves the sons of Israel, though they turn to other gods and love raisin cakes."** *[2] So I bought her for myself for fifteen shekels of silver and a homer and a half of barley (emphasis added).*

God asks Hosea not to retreat or isolate himself but to go and buy his adulteress wife back. That's a big ask. Would you be able to say "Yes" to it? Most would not. What an incredible moment! Here she is on the auction block in all her shame and loss. She is undoubtedly filled with regret for all that has been thrown away in her betrayal; in that moment of hopelessness, she sees her husband walk through the gates with a money purse and merchandise in his hand. Standing shackled, she sees through the crowd of people the man who took her in, loved her, fathered her children, and provided safety for her. She sees the one she betrayed, abandoned, and hurt making his way toward her. Why is he doing this? Is he here to see her shame fully realized as she is sold as a slave? Is he here for satisfaction, justice, or spite? To her amazement, he has come for something much more powerful.

As the bidding starts, Hosea lays down the largest offer. Paying more than others esteem her worthy of, this husband buys his unfaithful wife back to himself. He meets her betrayal with redemption. Just as God does His people. What a moment. What an incredible thing to say "Yes" to. Imagine what onlookers are thinking and saying of Hosea watching him buy back his unfaithful wife. Yet, he does it anyway. What an example for all believers. Right now, as you read this, what terrible thing is God asking you to meet with forgiveness and redemption? Ask Him to help you say "Yes" ...so everyone's chains can be loosed.

What Hosea does flies in the face of the enemy's lie that you can never trust anyone again. Just because one person betrays you is not a guarantee that others will. More than that, there is something greater here. He doesn't trust her. He doesn't have to. He trusts God. For Hosea, God is the trustworthy one. He's not taking a chance on Gomer; he's standing on God's promise. He chooses to walk in a courageous "Yes" to the Father. Not only does he ignore the enemy's lie, but he does what only he can do.

"Your promotion may come through answering the call to do something that no one else is willing to do."

Part of Hosea's and Joseph's stories is the simple fact that they answered a call no one else wanted a piece of. Many times, supernatural things require our participation. Dr. David Ford, in "Activating the Power of God", speaks to this issue:[6]

> *"Did God talk to others about fighting the giant before David showed up at the Israelite's camp? The whole Israel army could have responded, but they didn't. It was David who volunteered to face the giant. Your promotion may come through answering the call to do something that no one else is willing to do."*

The Truth: *You Can Trust God*

Look at a larger portion of the 1 Peter passage referred to earlier.

> *1 Peter 5:1-11 (NASB)*
> *[1] Therefore, I exhort the elders among you, as your fellow elder and witness of the sufferings of Christ, and a partaker also of the glory that is to be revealed, [2] shepherd the flock of God among you, exercising* **oversight not under compulsion, but voluntarily, according to**

*the will of God; and not for sordid gain, but with eagerness; ³ nor yet as lording it over those allotted to your charge, but proving to be examples to the flock. ⁴ And when the Chief Shepherd appears, you will receive the unfading crown of glory. ⁵ You younger men, likewise, be subject to your elders; and all of you, clothe yourselves with humility toward one another, for God is opposed to the proud, but gives grace to the humble. ⁶ Therefore humble yourselves under the mighty hand of God, that **He may exalt you at the proper time**, ⁷ casting all your anxiety on Him, because He cares for you. ⁸ Be of sober spirit, be on the alert. Your adversary, the devil, prowls around like a roaring lion, seeking someone to devour. ⁹ But resist him, firm in your faith, knowing that the same experiences of suffering are being accomplished by your brethren who are in the world. ¹⁰ **After you have suffered for a little while**, the God of all grace, who called you to His eternal glory in Christ, **<u>will Himself</u> perfect, confirm, strengthen and establish you.** ¹¹ To Him be dominion forever and ever. Amen (emphasis added).*

Peter points out something very important in this passage, which gives insight into the predatorial preferences of the enemy. In verse two, he reminds us that we are volunteers. We have signed up for this. God isn't forcing us to do anything, but if we choose to say "Yes" to Him, then it must be His terms, not ours. That's why it says, "According to the will of God..." This passage also serves as a reminder of, and even guarantees, suffering. Suffering is part of the journey of a believer. Moreover, we must humble ourselves. These are actions we don't really want to take. I certainly didn't want to humble myself and endure suffering! I wanted everything to be awesome. Without a willingness to humble themselves, a person will easily succumb to revenge, control, isolation, and other acts of the flesh.

The key to overcoming is revealed – it's found in humbling oneself. The reward is that God will exalt you at the proper time. You don't have to vindicate yourself or raise yourself up - He will do it for you, and it will be done at the right time, a moment you aren't qualified to determine. "After you have suffered for a little while, the God of all grace, who called you to His eternal glory in Christ, will Himself perfect, confirm, strengthen, and establish you." The truth is you don't have to be afraid of trusting others; you can trust God. You can even trust Him *in them.*

The Fruit: *Greater Relationship*

> ### Hosea 3:3-5 (NASB)
> [3] Then I said to her, "You shall stay with me for many days. You shall not play the harlot, nor shall you have a man; **so I will also be toward you.**" [4] For the sons of Israel will remain for many days without king or prince,

without sacrifice or sacred pillar and without ephod or household idols. ⁵ **Afterward the sons of Israel will return and seek the Lord their God** *and David their king; and* **they will come trembling to the Lord** *and to His goodness in the last days (emphasis added).*

Hosea reclaims his wife back while she receives her freedom and restoration to her household. Prophetically, Israel and God are once again reconciled. The fruit of enduring through betrayal is the restoration of the very thing the betrayal seeks to destroy - relationship. When you choose not to react in the flesh but to rather respond in the Spirit, you will build a deeper, more enduring relationship. Hillman writes of the various stages that Joseph goes through in his life and offers this astounding revelation of their purpose[7]:

> *The six stages of this process are designed to bring us to a place where God can fully trust us with all he wants to do in our lives. He knows he can trust us when we can glorify him in the process of the pain and suffering. If we fail to do this in our pit, then we will fail to glorify him in the elevation period. The truth is that if we walk away from God because of something bad that happens to us, then we never really had a relationship with him in the first place. God's goal is to make us servants, stewards, and slaves. And so the adversity period in our lives is designed to remove our*

dependence upon titles and accomplishments for our self-esteem. God brings us to the place where all we want is Christ in us in order to create Christ in others. That is when we know the testing has accomplished its purpose. God releases his blessing in proportion to the character you allow him to develop within you. He will totally ruin you and remake you at the same time. The result of this will be a new you, where you will be grateful to God for what he had done within you. Someday you will be able to say that you would actually go through the process again if it meant you would gain what you gained. God turns the pit into a well of the Holy Spirit—he makes a deposit that will last a lifetime.

Did you catch that? "God releases His character in proportion to the character you allow Him to develop within you." WOW! The amazing work God can do with your obedience in the face of the pain of broken trust is restoration and expansion, IN PROPORTION to the character He has developed within you. Look at what He did in Hosea 3. Israel was affected by one man's courageous "Yes". Who stands to benefit from your courageous "Yes"?

"God releases His character in proportion to the character you allow Him to develop within you."

In my case, I was the one who would gain the most by going through suffering. During a particularly difficult time of ministry, through the generosity of a friend, my wife and I went to a secluded cabin on a mountain in Colorado. I sat for three days. I was unable to do much because I was in such anguish over people who had left the church, what they were saying about me, and the financial strain of it all. On the fourth day, I decided to go fishing. I was really going to talk to God. I had not wanted to have the conversation the previous three days, but now we would have it out. I was angry; I was bitter; and I was exhausted. All I could find were worms and a little kid's *Barbie* rod and reel in the garage. I walked down to the river and still had enough spirituality in me to ask, "Where do you want me to fish today, Lord?" He said, "Right here. It's the only place you'll catch fish." Well...right here...was a stump with a gnarled weed of a tree on the left hand that blocked your view upstream. Behind me and slightly to the right was another large tree in the perfect spot to get tangled up on (as I did at least twelve times) as you drew back to cast. In front of me was a steep drop off except for what seemed to be Breer Rabbits' lost briar patch full of thorns. On my right was a beautiful view downstream and a deep and still area that anyone would recognize as the perfect spot to fish for trout. Obedient, yet frustrated, I sat down on the stump...fuming.

After a two-hour exercise in futility, a local woman that was out hiking passed by me. With a pitying look in her eye toward this poor tourist, she offered, "You know you're not going to catch anything here, right?" I said, "I'm not?" She said, "No, you need to fish down there. That's where the monsters are." She motioned toward the beautiful fishing hole that I longed for. I thanked her, and she went her way, probably wondering what I was doing in that bad spot casting a worm and cork in a river full of trout. She couldn't know that I was wondering the same thing. I looked like an idiot. And felt even more disgusted.

Before I could even get a word out, God asked me, "Do you know what your problem is?" As a professional spiritual leader, a Bible scholar, a man of prayer, and a pastor...I completely ignored the question. I had absolutely no desire to talk to Him about my problem. I wanted to talk to Him about the problem I had with Him! I asked Him if I could go fish where the monsters were. He told me I could, but that I wouldn't catch any fish. I wanted to know why, and He stated simply that this stump was where He told me to go, and that was the only place I would catch fish. But I wanted to go where the monsters were! For some reason, it felt like I was mic'd up. I could hear Him in real-time. Here's how this part of the conversation went:

> ME: "God, I want to fish over there where they are jumping out of the water."

> GOD: "You can."

> ME: "No, You said I can't."

> GOD: "No, I didn't."

> ME: "Yes, You did."

GOD: "No, I didn't. You asked me where I wanted you to fish, and I told you that this was the only place you'd catch anything. Do you know what your problem is?"

ME: (Again, ignoring the question.) "God, I want to go."

GOD: "Go ahead."

ME: "No, there will be a penalty."

GOD: "No. No penalty. Just no fish."

ME: "Ok. Well, I'm going."

GOD: "Ok, I'll see you over there."

And off I went. I had polarized lenses and could see these huge trout under the water. I even tried hitting them on the head with my worm and hook, but to no avail. One jumped out of the water, and it was gorgeous. I wanted it. I hit that one in the FACE at least six times. It would just swim around, come back, and bump my worm away with its nose. It was crazy. Not one nibble. I could hear the Lord asking me again if I knew what my problem was. I indignantly asked why I couldn't have that fish. He told me I could. I just needed to ask Him for it. So, I did. His reply was simple. "Go back to where I told you to fish."

Frustrated and mad, I packed my stuff up and went back to that stupid, worthless stump. As soon as I returned and tried to cast my bait, I got hung up in the tree again. It took twenty minutes to get it untangled, which was imperative since it was my only hook. At long last, when I finally got my bait in the river, that fish jumped out of the water several times in one beautiful arc after another until he was at my cork, and down it went. The drag wasn't right for this huge trout. I threw down the rod and grabbed the line in my hands. Gravity made me involuntarily rush down this steeply graded hill and right into the briar patch's thorns at the water's edge. Blood went down into my sock as I pulled the line by hand. Up and over the briar patch onto the bank, this monster flopped, and I pounced on top of him, getting my hand stuck with a fin. It was the most fun I have ever had catching a fish. That's when I opened up to the Lord.

I told Him how hurt I was, how frustrated I was, and how I couldn't understand His response to my obedience. He wanted to know what I wanted. I told him I wanted the church to be...more...more...successful. He inquired what I thought success was. I couldn't see what the problem was with an expanded scope of ministry, more opportunities for people to hear the Gospel, and more resources to lift judgment off of people. He said, "That's so beautiful. What do you mean by that?" I said, "More...uh...more...umm...more...moooore PEOPLE!" And there it was. He asked me again if I knew what my problem was. This time I bit. "What's my problem, God?" His reply changed my life.

"Do you really want an expanded scope of ministry so the Gospel can spread, or do you want a big church so people can come and see how awesome you are? Your problem, son, is that **you want to be great, and I am completely uninterested in that**. I want you to make my Son's name great in the earth. You proceed from a false premise. You believe that if you learn more, do better, preach better, be a better pastor, run faster, and jump higher, the church will grow. I am in charge of the size of your audience. It will be what I determine. Do you want me or not? Will you be content with doing only what I say? Are you content with just Me?"

I wept. I didn't know that was in me and didn't want it. He told me this fishing location was just like the town He called me to. It was inconvenient, hard, ill-equipped, and prone to pain and messes. But it would be where I would catch the monsters. I wanted to go where all my friends were and do what they did, but He had picked out a different spot for me. It was a place of suffering, and it would cure me of the need to be awesome. God is awesome, and no one else.

My problem was that I wanted to be great, but God was completely uninterested in that.

My problem was that I wanted to be great, but God had no interest in that. He wants me to make His Son's name famous in the earth. It's not about me. You see, I thought the monsters worth catching in ministry were a larger platform, a bigger audience, influence, and success. Those are not the monsters in God's estimation. He wanted me to catch humility, servanthood, death to self, total dependence on Him, and radical obedience regardless of whether or not it benefitted me. He chose this difficult place and hard ground to help shape me more and more into the image of Christ.

It is through the fellowship of His sufferings that we come to know the power of His resurrection (Philippians 3:10). From that little Charlie Brown Christmas tree of a fishing spot, I out-fished everyone on the mountain that day. And the monster I caught with his head and tail cut off was still too big to fit diagonally in my 13x9 pan! It's only through suffering that I would allow God to bring me to a place where He could fully trust me with all He had promised in my life. I had to learn to glorify Him in times of pain and loss, not just on the mountaintop moments.

Many times, we go through things that we wouldn't choose, but God uses them for our good. While we don't have to stay in these places forever, the wilderness is a necessary part of the journey to the Promised Land. Trust Him. He's working for your good.

CHAPTER 5

In the Middle of Bondage

GOD'S METHOD ALWAYS SEEMS to be vision first and then reality. So many mistake the vision for the reality, but in between the vision and the reality there is often a deep valley of humiliation. . . How often has a faithful soul plunged into a like darkness; after the vision has come the test and the darkness.[8]

The Reality of God's Favor

Bondage is a roller coaster ride.

Joseph's story is a tragedy thus far. He has so much promise yet has lost so much. His mother, Rachel, died while giving birth to his younger brother, Benjamin. His brothers have disowned him and sold him into slavery; his father doesn't even know to look for him because he believes he is dead; and now, he is in a foreign land with language barriers that prohibit communication and no friends to speak of. It seems that his dreams will never be fulfilled. Bondage is such a roller coaster ride. There are always highs and lows in bondage. Whether it comes in the form of addiction or other ways, being bound to something offers a wide range of emotions. I've heard from individuals in addiction counseling how, after some of their lowest moments, there are periods—sometimes days, weeks, months, or even years—of what feels like freedom, only to be followed by relapse, which brings even greater shame and destruction. It is the same with Joseph.

Genesis 39 (NASB)
*¹ Now Joseph had been taken down to Egypt; and Potiphar, an Egyptian officer of Pharaoh, the captain of the bodyguard, bought him from the Ishmaelites, who had taken him down there. ² **The Lord was with Joseph, so he became a successful man.** And he was in the house of his master, the Egyptian. ³ Now his master saw that the Lord was with him and how the Lord caused all that he did to prosper in his hand. ⁴ So Joseph found favor in his sight and became his personal servant; and he made him overseer over his house, and all that he owned he put in his charge. ⁵ It came about that from the time he made him overseer in his house and over all that he owned, the Lord blessed the Egyptian's house on account of Joseph; thus the Lord's blessing was upon all that he owned, in the house and in the field. ⁶ So he left everything he owned in Joseph's charge; and with him there he did not concern*

himself with anything except the food which he
ate (emphasis added).

Joseph is a slave, but he prospers in his bondage. He becomes ruler of his master's house, and everything he touches seems to flourish. Here's the problem with that. He is still a slave. And a slave who is a blessing to his master's house, while he may gain some additional freedoms, is not soon to be released. The part I struggle with the most is that my definition of favor looks different than God's definition. Joseph has favor at every turn. God's favor makes him the son of a barren wife, the answer to a decades-old prayer. God's favor turns him from a potential murder victim into a living slave. God's favor prospers everything Joseph touches as a slave, and His favor is noticed by his master, who gives him control over his whole affairs. In prison, he will also have favor, but again...I come to my dilemma. I don't want "slave favor". I want to NOT BE A SLAVE. I don't want "dungeon favor" ...I WANT OUT OF THE DUNGEON! Keep your favor God...just let me be normal.

The Problem: *Bondage, Prosperity, and False Accusation*

Genesis 39:6-20 (NASB)
⁶ So he left everything he owned in Joseph's charge; and with him there he did not concern himself with anything except the food which he ate. Now Joseph was handsome in form and

appearance. [7] It came about after these events that his master's wife looked with desire at Joseph, and she said, "Lie with me." [8] But he refused and said to his master's wife, "Behold, with me here, my master does not concern himself with anything in the house, and he has put all that he owns in my charge. [9] There is no one greater in this house than I, and he has withheld nothing from me except you, because you are his wife. How then could I do this great evil and sin against God?" [10] As she spoke to Joseph day after day, he did not listen to her to lie beside her or be with her. [11] Now it happened one day that he went into the house to do his work, and none of the men of the household was there inside. [12] She caught him by his garment, saying, "Lie with me!" And he left his garment in her hand and fled, and went outside. [13] When she saw that he had left his garment in her hand and had fled outside, [14] she called to the men of her household and said to them, "See, he has brought in a Hebrew to us to make sport of us; he came in to me to lie with me, and I screamed. [15] When he heard that I raised my voice and screamed, he left his garment beside me and fled and went outside." [16] So she left his garment beside her until his master came home. [17] Then she spoke to him with these words, "The Hebrew slave, whom you brought to us, came in to me to make sport of me; [18] and as I raised my voice and screamed, he left his garment beside me and fled outside." [19] *Now* **when his master heard the words of his wife,** *which she spoke to him, saying, "This is what your slave did to me," his anger burned.* [20] *So* **Joseph's master took him and put him into the jail,** *the place where the king's prisoners were confined; and he was there in the jail (emphasis added).*

Joseph begins this part of the story as a slave. God blesses him, and he becomes powerful. He is put in charge of everything. All that he does prospers. Potiphar's wife is attracted to him physically and most likely is intrigued by his success. She tries to seduce him, but he refuses. This is usually the end of most stories. Temptation is a powerful foe that must be conquered again and again.

Dietrich Bonhoeffer was a German pastor and exceptional theologian. Living during the rise of Hitler and the Third Reich, he also became part of the resistance and ultimately was martyred on April 9, 1945, when he was executed by the Nazis. He was just thirty-nine years old, and as great as his surviving works are, what he called his greatest work was destroyed in a concentration camp. Yet, in a small booklet entitled *Temptation*, he gives an intriguing explanation of how temptation impacts us[9]:

In our members there is a slumbering inclination towards desire which is both sudden and fierce. With irresistible power desire seizes mastery over the flesh. All at once a secret, smouldering fire is kindled. The flesh burns and is in flames. It makes no difference whether it is sexual desire, or ambition, or vanity, or desire for revenge, or love of fame and power, or greed for money, or, finally, that strange desire for the beauty of the world, of nature. Joy in God is in course of being extinguished in us and we seek all our joy in the creature. At this moment God is quite unreal to us, he loses all reality, and only desire for the creature is real; the only reality is the devil. Satan does not here fill us with hatred of God, but with forgetfulness of God. . . The lust thus aroused envelops the mind and will of man in deepest darkness. The powers of clear discrimination and of decision are taken from us. . . It is here that everything within me rises up against the Word of God.

Charles Swindoll offers more insight into this moment Joseph must face, as do all of us[10]:

There is not a person who has cast his shadow across this earth, including Jesus Christ, who has not faced temptation. And there is not a single person who has ever lived, except Christ, who has not yielded to it at one time or another and suffered the consequences. Temptation is an inevitable part of our fallen world. We cannot escape it. Temptation also wears many faces. There is, for example, material temptation, which is the lust for things. It might be as big as a house or as small as a ring. It might be as bright and dazzling as a brand-new Porsche or as dull and dusty as an antique roll-top desk. Yet, who hasn't felt the burning passion of lust for things? And who hasn't at times yielded to it unwisely? Then there is what we will call personal temptation, which is the lust for fame, for authority, for power, or control over others. It might be as simple as lust for a title like "CEO" or "president" or "doctor" or "professor" or "admiral." There is nothing wrong with those titles or those positions, until lust comes and says, "You deserve that, for what it will mean to you." Finally, there is sensual temptation, which is lust for another person—or, in reality, lust for the person's body. I'm referring here to the hedonistic desire to have and enjoy that which is not one's own, either legally or morally.

Because Joseph engaged in battle with this third category of temptation, we shall limit our thoughts in this chapter to that particular one. As we do, let's not forget Bonhoeffer's very practical reminder that when we yield to that particular temptation, "the powers of clear discrimination and of decision are taken from us".

There isn't much text given to the internal struggle Joseph may or may not feel, but as a man, he certainly has to battle it. What we do know is that he battles it successfully. His integrity is intact, but Potiphar's wife decides to falsely accuse him. Now, instead of being a slave in a household, he is a prisoner in the dungeon.

Who we are is more important than *where* we are.

The highs and lows continue to roll. It may seem, at first glance, that even though Joseph doesn't yield to temptation, his powers of decision-making are still taken from him. But as we look deeper, we may find that to be untrue. Joseph may not have any say about where he will live (in a dungeon), but he is the one who determines who he is. For Joseph, and for us, *who* we are is more important than *where* we are. The enemy may do things to us, but only we have the power to determine who we are as an individual.

It is important to remember that God has a perspective that Joseph lacks. Unlike us humans, who tend to focus on the present, God sees the end from the beginning. We often receive a call or dream from God, believing that the incredible nature of that vision reflects the entire journey ahead. However, when that journey becomes challenging or feels completely opposite to the joy and wonder of the dream, we may become convinced that God will never fulfill His promise. In these moments, we might see only our current circumstances, which can lead to doubt. But it is important to remember to see things from God's perspective.

Consider what Os Hillman wrote[11]:

As a young man, Joseph had a sense of his destiny. God often gives us a picture of our future so that we will remember this picture when we are being tested. This is so that we can trust him in the valleys. However, this usually doesn't reveal how God intends to bring about his purpose in our lives. It is important to understand that none of us really derive the character qualities God desires for our lives while we are on the mountain. It is in the valley where the fruit is planted and harvested. Fruit cannot grow on the mountain; it must grow in the valley. God is a God of the mountains, but he is even more a God of the valleys. In the valley, it is more difficult to see ahead; the clouds often cover the valley and limit our sight. Joseph was thrust into a deep valley that left him wondering if the God of his fathers had forsaken him. Jesus hoped that he might be able to avoid the valley that caused him to sweat drops of blood, hoping there would be another way besides going to the cross. There is a valley that each of us must enter, usually unwillingly, in order to experience the God of the valley—and to experience his faithfulness in the valleys. Once we have spent time in the valley, we come out with something we would have never gained if we had not entered it in the first place. The valley brings much fruit into our lives so that we might plant seeds into the lives of others. God does not waste valley experiences. If we are faithful in the valley, then we will enter a new dimension with God that we never thought possible. There is a harvest of wisdom and virtue that can only be grown in the valley. The apostle Paul understood this process when he wrote:

We are troubled on every side, yet not distressed; we are perplexed, but not in despair; persecuted, but not forsaken; cast down, but not might be made manifest in our body. For we which live are always delivered unto death for Jesus' sake, that the life also of Jesus might be made manifest in our mortal flesh. So then death worketh in us, but life in you. (2 Corinthians 4:8–12, KJV)

It is important that we do not extricate ourselves out of our valley experience. If you advance yourself before it is time, then it will result in leanness in your soul. Our timetable for advancement out of the valley is dependent on our obedience in the valley. God doesn't measure timetables; he measures growth. The Israelites were supposed to enter the Promised Land in only twelve days. However, their disobedience kept them in the desert for forty years!

*If you extricate yourself out of the valley before it is time,
then it will result in leanness in your soul.*

Real fruitfulness requires going through the valley. If you want to experience abundance in your life, you must embark on the journey through your personal valleys. This journey isn't always easy, but God promises it will be worth it. Like Joseph, who was a slave, dealing with bondage can make it hard to envision a day of freedom, let alone one of authority. No matter how it may have felt for him or how you might feel right now, the truth is that bondage is always temporary.

The Lie: *You Will Never be Free*

When we are in the middle of bondage, it is easy to believe the lie of the enemy that we will always be enslaved to whatever seems to have a hold on us. Hopelessness creeps in, and the lie feels convincing, appearing to have all the evidence stacked on its side. Nothing around us suggests that freedom is on the way to liberate us from our chains. It's gone from bad to worse. Why should tomorrow be any different? This perspective overlooks the power of God and His ability to break the chains that have bound us. As Proverbs 13:12 reminds us, "Hope deferred makes the heart sick." There came a day when the children of Israel would become a prime example of this.

Generations after Joseph rises to the position of second-in-command to Pharaoh, a new Pharaoh comes to power—one who neither recognizes Joseph's legacy nor respects his people. Driven by fear of their increasing population, he enslaves them, catapulting an entire people group into bondage and forced labor. As days pass, then years, and eventually generations, babies are born into captivity, marked with a slave identity from birth.

Imagine inheriting slavery as your legacy. You have suffered through it your entire life. Before you, your father was a slave, and his father was a slave, just as his father was. You've heard of a time when your people were free, but generations have passed since that time. You've never known autonomy and your mindset has been trained to believe that you never will. Then, a seemingly crazy Egyptian prince claiming to be one of you appears out of the wilderness and tells the most powerful man on Earth to let you and all your kin go free. It would be hard to believe and much harder to actually expect to be set free. And yet, it happens. But, before it does, things get even more bizarre. God, through Moses, performs apocalyptic-type signs and wonders in the land, causing Pharaoh to relent. He releases the children of Israel to leave Egypt as free people. They even request gold from their captors and actually receive it! Slavery has ended after 400 years. It is an 'and suddenly' type of moment.

Imagine that you, your family, and everyone you've ever known pack it all up and head out of town, feeling a liberty you have never known. But then you arrive at the Red Sea, an insurmountable barrier between you and your ultimate freedom. If that is not enough to trigger the "We'll always be slaves" mentality, you look up to see your cousin shouting, "The Egyptians are coming!" It turns out that Pharaoh decides his change of heart is only a moment of temporary insanity, as he quickly realizes that freeing hundreds of thousands of slaves, who provide free labor, would be a disastrous decision for his economy. Not to mention, the last plague claimed the life of his beloved son, so he's got a score to settle.

Now, with a vengeful king commanding the mightiest army in the history of the world breathing down your neck, you find yourself led by "God", through this guy Moses, into a valley with impassable mountains on either side to an un-crossable Red Sea. The army is behind you, the mountains on either side of you, and the Red Sea in front of you. Death seems to be at hand, and the voice of the serpent is in your ears, hissing, "You will NEVER be free!" The slave in you cries out, "Were there not enough graves in Egypt that you have brought us out here to die?" The problem isn't leaving Egypt. The real problem is getting Egypt out of you. In his book on healing, John Proodian points out how we should respond to the promise of yesterday[12]:

> *There is a biblical principle to this concept that God has already accomplished something we need to enter into now. For example, the Israelites didn't enter into the promised land until forty years later than God intended. Their inheritance was supposed to be received at that time, but hesitation and unbelief hindered God's now plan for four decades. They wandered around in the wilderness and God had planned for them to take possession of the land at that moment. Your provision of*

healing isn't something that is coming to you in the future. It was there before you were. What we need to do is take yesterday's truth and make it today's reality.

Regardless of the challenges you face, you can trust in God's Word. It existed long before you did. A slave mentality can lead you to believe that God has abandoned you, leaving you in a dead-end situation. It may try to persuade you that your freedom is just an illusion and that God, in His cruelty, intends to lead you to ruin. This mentality seeks to make you forget God's promises. This is one reason why the events described in Exodus 5-14 remain relevant today.

This pervasive notion that you are always going to be a slave to fear, control, lust, greed, or substances is a lie. No matter how strong your chains may seem, they are not more powerful than God. While they may feel powerful to you, they hold no power over Him. The Red Sea and Pharaoh's army are not obstacles for God. The real question is, "Do you trust God?" What appears to be a dead end leading to your destruction is actually an opportunity for God to reveal His glory! Stand still and witness the salvation of the Lord!

What we view as terminal, God views as transitional!"

Isn't God's power over death the miraculous part of Jesus' crucifixion and resurrection? A mentor of mine, Pastor Tom Sterbens, once texted me, **"What we view** as terminal, God views as transitional!" It's better to receive God's miraculous provision than to have everything go according to my own plans without any difficulties. I would choose the parting of the Red Sea any day over my own plans. His way is far more amazing! Most of the time, the excruciating pain of our circumstances leads us to false conclusions. But I promise you that God is working for your good, transitioning you from bondage to freedom, from death to life. That's the truth.

The Truth: *Truth Makes You Free*

If Joseph's story has a familiar ring to it, consider another descendant of Jacob whose claims of future exaltation were considered arrogant. Jesus was sent to the other sons of Jacob (Israel) because of their Father's compassion, but his Jewish brothers plotted to seize him and kill him. He too was sold for pieces of silver, his coat was stripped from his back, he was cast into an empty grave that would not hold him for long, and then all Israel sat down to eat. (Jesus was crucified immediately before Jews celebrated the Passover meal.) And just as Joseph saved Egypt from famine, Jesus was sent to save Gentiles until the time of Israel's repentance, when, according to prophecy, the sons of Jacob will finally bow before him.[13]

Jesus certainly has something to say about being bound to your circumstances or becoming free in Him. Freedom isn't really about choosing for yourself; it's fundamentally about truth. On His way to Galilee, Jesus travels through Samaria and meets a woman known as the Samaritan woman. Her life is entrenched with one mistake after another, leaving her too embarrassed to draw water from the well when other women are present. Trapped in a cycle of broken relationships, burdened by guilt, and overwhelmed by shame, she makes the journey to the well alone to avoid others. Little does she know her next encounter will be with a Man unlike any she has ever met—a Man who can satisfy her thirsty soul so that she will never thirst again. The Samaritan woman meets Jesus while trying to escape social stigma, and the first thing He does is lead her to a place of truth.

John 4:7-26 (NASB)

7 There came a woman of Samaria to draw water. Jesus said to her, "Give Me a drink." 8 For His disciples had gone away into the city to buy food. 9 Therefore the Samaritan woman said to Him, "How is it that You, being a Jew, ask me for a drink since I am a Samaritan woman?" (For Jews have no dealings with Samaritans.) 10 Jesus answered and said to her, "If you knew the gift of God, and who it is who says to you, 'Give Me a drink,' you would have asked Him, and He would have given you living water." 11 She said to Him, "Sir, You have nothing to draw with and the well is deep; where then do You get that living water? [12] *You are not greater than our father Jacob, are You, who gave us the well, and drank of it himself and his sons and his cattle?"* [13] *Jesus answered and said to her, "Everyone who drinks of this water will thirst again;* [14] *but whoever drinks of the water that I will give him shall never thirst; but the water that I will give him will become in him a well of water springing up to eternal life."* [15] *The woman said to Him, "Sir, give me this water, so I will not be thirsty nor come all the way here to draw."* [16] *He said to her, "Go, call your husband and come here."* [17] *The woman answered and said, "I have no husband." Jesus said to her, "You have correctly said, 'I have no husband';* [18] *for you have had five husbands, and the one whom you now have is not your husband; this you have said truly."* [19] *The woman said to Him, "Sir, I perceive that You are a prophet.* [20] *Our fathers worshiped in this mountain, and you people say that in Jerusalem is the place where men ought to worship."* [21] *Jesus said to her, "Woman, believe Me, an hour is coming when neither in this mountain nor in Jerusalem will you worship the Father.* [22] *You worship what you do not know; we worship what we know, for salvation is from the Jews.* [23] *But an hour is coming, and now is, when the true worshipers will worship the Father in spirit and truth; for such people the Father seeks to be His worshipers.* ²⁴ *God is spirit, and those who worship Him must worship in spirit and truth." * ²⁵ *The woman said to Him, "I know that Messiah is coming (He who is called Christ); when that One comes, He will declare all things to us." * ²⁶ *Jesus said to her, "I who speak to you am He."*

Pastor Tom Sterbens has taught this passage for years. I have come to know it by heart. His insight into what truth really means is astounding[14]:

The Greek root of the word "truth" is lanthano from which we derive terms such as latent, concealed, and hidden or to hide. Aletheia is a negated form of that word from which we get truth or reality, but in the simplest of senses it would mean, not-latent, not-concealed, not-hidden or unhidden.

What a powerful connotation as John would write of the incarnation of Jesus Christ, "And the Word became flesh, and dwelt among us, and we saw His glory, glory as of the only begotten from the Father, full of grace and truth," (John 1:14 NASB). Jesus came into this world full of grace and truth. Full of grace and unhidden-ness. Jesus was the great "un-hider!" He did not come to "unhide" sin just for the sake of exposing people, but He came to call us out from the places we hide and into the "reality" of His Holy presence.

In the Garden of Eden, mankind listened to the whisper of a lie, rejected God's Word and worth, and the first thing they did was "hide." The words still carry a haunting echo and curse on mankind, "I was afraid...so I hid" (cf. Gen. 3:10). With the advent of Jesus Christ, the God of Holy, who is the God of Love, reaches to mankind and announces, "You were still too afraid to come out of hiding into the reality of My Presence so I have come, and I have come full of grace and unhidden-ness. I am the great un-hider!"

So there this woman at the well stands, trapped in a life that is out of control and beyond her control and yet unaware she is in the presence of God-the-Holy, the God of Love in the flesh, and she begins "peeking" out from behind the pain of her hiding place. (Adapted Version)

Jesus asks her, "Will you give me a drink?" (John 4:7, NIV). This seemingly insignificant question cuts to the core of her being. Going to the well daily represents her source of provision and the promise of tomorrow. Giving away her provision could lead to more effort, work, or a shortage. Remember, the orphan spirit often protects and provides for itself.

> Jesus comes into our lives to bring freedom
> and, instead, we meet Him with all the reasons
> why we can't be free.

The Samaritan responds to Truth with reason and rationalizing. How often do we follow a similar pattern? Jesus comes into our lives to bring freedom and, instead, we meet Him with all the reasons why we can't be free.

Jesus begins speaking a language she has never heard before...living water. Given her current circumstances, this concept is likely foreign to her. Once again, she meets Truth with doubt and reasoning. The woman begins to question who He is (vs. 12) and how this can be possible. Jesus offers Himself as Truth by inviting her to partake of living water. He describes water that will enable her to never be thirsty again...He invites her to partake of Him, the living water. Jesus knows that everything she has ever needed can be found in Him.

In the second Truth encounter, Jesus asks the woman to call for her husband (John 4:16-17), and she readily admits that she has no husband. This singular decision to be honest and transparent marks the beginning of her journey toward freedom. Jesus is aware of her sins and the brokenness in her life. While He does not need her to confess, she needs to embrace Truth in order to be free. Jesus promises her that this living water will provide a wellspring of eternal life (John 4:14). Her choice to be open and not hide her reality is life-giving for her and for anyone else she might come into contact with.

Tom Sterbens further notes[15]:

Don't miss those first words, "I...I...I...uh...I don't have a husband." And Jesus replies, "This you have said TRULY." Do you see it? "This you have said, un-hidden!" Now watch the conversation as something in her begins to awaken, something long lost in the Garden of Eden, something of two worlds meeting as the "Spirit" of God intersects with the "spirit" of mankind who is willing to step out of hiding into the unhidden-ness of truth. Do not miss the language here as it bridges time and space and meets us today in our world:

The woman (vs. 20): *"What should I do now, how do I worship, where do I worship, with what style do I worship?"*

Jesus (vs. 21-23): *"That's really not the issue, people have lots of ideas about worship, about where you should worship and how you should worship. But a time is coming, as a matter of fact for you the time is right now, because there is really only one kind of worshipper, and that is a 'true,' unhidden worshiper who will allow their worth to be shaped by the Father as they stand in the Spirit in total unhidden-ness! These are the only people God encounters. These are the only people He seeks. True worshipers are unhidden worshipers. There is no other kind."*

For such the Father seeks! As a note, this verse has often been used to represent a "needy God," who is out searching for someone to worship Him, and that certainly is not what Jesus is saying. He is responding to the question of the woman concerning where and how she should worship. Jesus informs her the Father only seeks or encounters one kind of worshipper—one who is unhidden. (Adapted Version)

In this final encounter with Truth, Jesus invites the Samaritan woman to a new understanding of worship. He begins by saying, "Believe me, a time is coming" (John 4:21). This new place of worship requires both spirit and truth—encompassing both the little "s" of spirit, which represents the heart of who she is, and the big "S" of Spirit, signifying the Holy Spirit. Jesus calls the woman to worship authentically, coming before the Lord openly and without concealment.

Furthermore, He calls her to worship in the Spirit and through the Spirit of Truth. The Samaritan woman experiences this truth directly in verses 24 and 25 when she proclaims, "I know that Messiah is coming." Jesus then responds confidently, "I am He." In this moment, the Samaritan woman truly encounters *The Truth*.

When God comes near, our only response should be that of being undone and unhidden.

The Father is seeking those who will choose to worship Him in spirit and in truth. Often, we approach the Lord while resisting the light of truth that seeks to illuminate our darkness. However, this is how we truly begin to worship in spirit. We must align ourselves with the Spirit of God, allowing our spirit to dictate our responses to a holy God instead of letting our flesh take control. When God comes near, full of grace and truth, our only response should be that of being undone and unhidden. Let's take it even further.

The Fruit: *Choosing a New Father*

John 8:31-47 (NASB)
[31] So Jesus was saying to those Jews who had believed Him, "If you continue in My word, then you are truly disciples of Mine; [32] and **you will know the truth, and the truth will make you free."** *[33] They answered Him,* **"We are Abraham's descendants and have never yet been enslaved to anyone; how is it that You say, 'You will become free'?"** *[34] Jesus answered them, "Truly, truly, I say to you,* **everyone who commits sin is the slave of sin. [35] The slave does not remain in the house forever; the son does remain forever. [36] So if the Son makes you free, you will be free indeed.** *[37] I know that you are Abraham's descendants; yet you seek to kill Me, because*

My word has no place in you. ³⁸ **I speak the things which I have seen with My Father; therefore you also do the things which you heard from your father."** ³⁹ *They answered and said to Him,* **"Abraham is our father." Jesus said to them, "If you are Abraham's children, do the deeds of Abraham.** ⁴⁰ *But as it is, you are seeking to kill Me, a man who has told you the truth, which I heard from God; this Abraham did not do.* ⁴¹ *You are doing the deeds of your father." They said to Him, "We were not born of fornication; we have one Father: God."* ⁴² *Jesus said to them,* **"If God were your Father, you would love Me,** *for I proceeded forth and have come from God, for I have not even come on My own initiative, but He sent Me.* ⁴³ *Why do you not understand what I am saying? It is because you cannot hear My word.* ⁴⁴ **You are of your father the devil, and you want to do the desires of your father.** *He was a murderer from the beginning, and does not stand in the truth because there is no truth in him. Whenever he speaks a lie, he speaks from his own nature, for he is a liar and the father of lies.* ⁴⁵ *But because I speak the truth, you do not believe Me.* ⁴⁶ *Which one of you convicts Me of sin? If I speak truth, why do you not believe Me?* ⁴⁷ **He who is of God hears the words of God; for this reason you do not hear them, because you are not of God"** *(emphasis added).*

In this passage, Jesus seeks to define what true freedom is and the results it brings. He states that "the truth will make you free" (verse 32). Do you notice the connection between truth and freedom? Often, truth is seen merely as being "right." When we discuss truth, we frequently focus on determining who is right and who is wrong. However, this often relates more to facts than to genuine truth. Jesus is concerned with something much more significant: freedom. He wants to identify who is truly free and who remains a slave. In the verses above, the Jews' response reveals that they are still enslaved by sin, resulting in a loss of their sonship. However, if the Son *MAKES* you free, you are genuinely free. You haven't busted out of jail only to be on the run looking over your shoulder; you've been pardoned and no one has the authority to bind you again. Do you see the difference?

> The test of truth is freedom and
> the test of freedom is truth.

The Jews respond to Jesus by highlighting their lineage from Abraham, essentially saying, "Abraham is our Daddy!" Jesus counters by pointing out that their actions do not reflect that of their father. If they truly are Abraham's children, they would love Jesus. He goes further by explaining that sons inherit the traits of their fathers. To identify someone's father, one can simply evaluate their actions. So, ask yourself: do your choices, behavior, and words reflect your Heavenly Father? If we are indeed children of our Heavenly Father, we will forgive, love, and show kindness and goodness, rather than engage in the works of the flesh. We will be free from retribution, control, fear, and similar burdens. This is simply because the test of truth is freedom, and the test of freedom is truth.

> *Genesis 39:21-23 (NASB)*
> *[21] But the Lord was with Joseph and extended kindness to him, and gave him favor in the sight of the chief jailer. [22] The chief jailer committed to Joseph's charge all the prisoners who were in the jail; so that whatever was done there, he was responsible for it. [23] The chief jailer did not supervise anything under Joseph's charge because the Lord was with him; and whatever he did, the Lord made to prosper (emphasis added).*

Unlike biological fathers, we have the ability to choose our spiritual father. The reward for overcoming our bondage is receiving a true father. Joseph is blessed regardless of his circumstances because he is certain of his Heavenly Father's love, which gives him a strong sense of identity. This raises an important question: "Who's your daddy?" Choosing our spiritual father can be one of life's greatest gifts, or at the very least, a significant relief. While earthly fathers may have good intentions, they are still human and can fall short. In contrast, our Heavenly Father is perfect and cannot disappoint us.

God's purpose for me isn't dependent
on my performance or other's opinions.
This is radical and revolutionary.

When I receive my identity, purpose, and perspective from my Heavenly Father, it transforms how I perceive others and experience what happens around me or to me. What a gift! I don't have to perform or seek perfection to get approval...I know I am His son, in whom He is well pleased. It is not because of my deeds, but simply because of whose I am. He's my Dad, and He loves me. He will correct me without condemnation, altering my perception of my struggles. God's purpose for me isn't dependent on my performance or other's opinions, so what they say or do is immaterial. This is radical and revolutionary.

Even though Joseph is being tested and tossed about from one trial to another, his relationship with the Heavenly Father acts as a shield around him. Have you noticed the favor he experiences wherever he goes? Can you relate to this in your own life? In many ways, things might seem terrible. They are not what you would have chosen, and you may be unsure why this is happening or when it will end. Yet, right in the midst of these difficulties, you can also experience favor. God may open doors for you, bless you in remarkable ways, or bring about situations that are clearly supernatural.

Why does this happen? God does not promise that we will be free from trials or testing, but He does promise to be with us throughout these challenges. When you have a relationship with Him, you also receive His favor, even in the toughest times.

Jesus is certainly favored by God but still had to go through rejection, betrayal, and death. In addition to the shield of faith, David describes another form of protection in Psalm 5:22: "For you, O Lord, will bless the righteous with favor. You will surround him as with a shield." This favor is not simply a pleasant mist from heaven that prevents bad things from happening. Here, the Word tells us that God's favor is a shield that covers and protects. And I would remind you that the only place you need a shield is in battle.

Joseph needs the favor of God, not when he receives his coat of many colors but when the fight for his life, his integrity, and his freedom are in peril. Joseph knows all too well that God's favor is a shield protecting us from the attack of the enemy, not some goose-pimply fairy dust that keeps us comfortable. This is a huge benefit when we choose God as our Father. We get access to His shield of favor—the type of favor that makes murderous brothers change their minds, masters put a slave in charge of the whole house, and a jailor to give authority to a prisoner. It can make our enemies be at peace with us right in the middle of our story.

CHAPTER 6

In the Middle of Neglect

JOSEPH'S STORY NOW TAKES a sorrowful and all too familiar turn. Have you ever done one good thing after another without reward? It can be demoralizing. Even though Joseph has found favor in prison, he remains in the dungeon. His most comfortable cage is still just that—a cage. Then something interesting happens. Two men from Pharaoh's inner circle are imprisoned and subsequently need spiritual interpretations of their dreams. Guess who God gives the ability and favor to interpret for them. Yep, our main man, Joseph. If all goes well, it might lead to finding favor with Pharaoh and getting out of this unjust incarceration. But that would be too easy...

The Problem: *Forgotten and Disregarded*

Up to this point in Joseph's life, his entire family had seen the favor of his father, and Egyptians had seen the favor of his God. But what kind of favor? Potiphar recognized that God was with Joseph while knowing that he'd been sold as a slave. The head jailer saw that God was with Joseph while knowing that he'd been thrown into prison. They couldn't have seen an unknown God in the circumstances in which they first encountered Joseph, so they must have seen it in his more enduring characteristics. And even in the eyes of ancient Egyptians, it was obvious that divine favor and easy circumstances were not by any means synonymous. That's true for us as well. We are divinely favored in Christ, blessed with the unimaginable glory of knowing him and sharing his inheritance. Yet life is sometimes mercilessly difficult. That wasn't a contradiction in Joseph's life, and it's not a contradiction in ours. If our difficulties were eternal and our blessings temporary, we wouldn't consider ourselves the subjects of God's favor. But for us, the situation is reversed. The trials are temporary, and the blessings are eternal.[16]

Most of the time, while we are in the middle of neglect, trial, and affliction, we do not see or feel like we are walking in God's favor. Take Joseph's story, for example—what seems favorable about being betrayed by family, sold as a slave, falsely accused, and living in bondage? During my most difficult trials, I felt sure that everyone else viewed my life and ministry as a failure, just as I did. How could they not? Problems arose one after another, and I felt like a mess trying to handle it all. The stress and pressure of leading while feeling powerless were overwhelming. I remember telling one pastor who became my friend during this time, "Man, I wish you could have known me when my life was awesome. I don't know why you are even my friend!"

> Life can be a series of uncontrollable circumstances that have nothing to do with a person's worth.

I used to look down on people who were going from problem to problem, thinking to myself... "Get your life together, man!" Now, I understand that life can be a series of uncontrollable circumstances that have nothing to do with a person's worth. The truth is that others can more easily recognize the favor of God in a person's life than we can in our own. As stated above, everyone in Joseph's life could see God's favor no matter his circumstances. Whether he was a slave or a prisoner...it didn't take them long to recognize that God was with this guy.

What does that mean for you? What signs of favor are you overlooking right now that God is performing in your life? Can you shift your focus from what is wrong to what is praiseworthy, as mentioned in Philippians 4:8? Regardless of what you are going through, remember one of the most reassuring phrases in Scripture is "It came to pass." In other words, this situation won't last forever.

Genesis 40:1-23 (NASB)
1 *Then it came about after these things, the*

cupbearer and the baker for the king of Egypt offended their lord, the king of Egypt. [2] Pharaoh was furious with his two officials, the chief cupbearer and the chief baker. [3] So he put them in confinement in the house of the captain of the bodyguard, in the jail, the same place where Joseph was imprisoned. [4] The captain of the bodyguard put Joseph in charge of them, and he took care of them; and they were in confinement for some time. [5] Then the cupbearer and the baker for the king of Egypt, who were confined in jail, both had a dream the same night, each man with his own dream and each dream with its own interpretation. [6] When Joseph came to them in the morning and observed them, behold, they were dejected. [7] He asked Pharaoh's officials who were with him in confinement in his master's house, "Why are your faces so sad today?" [8] Then they said to him, "We have had a dream and there is no one to interpret it." **Then Joseph said to them, "Do not interpretations belong to God?** *Tell it to me, please." [9] So the chief cupbearer told his dream to Joseph, and said to him, "In my dream, behold, there was a vine in front of me; [10] and on the vine were three branches. And as it was budding, its blossoms came out, and its clusters produced ripe grapes. [11] Now Pharaoh's cup was in my hand; so I took the grapes and squeezed them into Pharaoh's cup, and I put the cup into Pharaoh's hand." [12] Then*

Joseph said to him, "This is the interpretation of it: the three branches are three days; 13 within three more days Pharaoh will lift up your head and restore you to your office; and you will put Pharaoh's cup into his hand according to your former custom when you were his cupbearer. 14 Only keep me in mind when it goes well with you, and please do me a kindness by mentioning me to Pharaoh and get me out of this house. 15 For I was in fact kidnapped from the land of the Hebrews, and even here I have done nothing that they should have put me into the dungeon." 16 When the chief baker saw that he had interpreted favorably, he said to Joseph, "I also saw in my dream, and behold, there were three baskets of white bread on my head; 17 and in the top basket there were some of all sorts of baked food for Pharaoh, and the birds were eating them out of the basket on my head." 18 Then Joseph answered and said, "This is its interpretation: the three baskets are three days; 19 within three more days Pharaoh will lift up your head from you and will hang you on a tree, and the birds will eat your flesh off you." 20 Thus it came about on the third day, which was Pharaoh's birthday, that he made a feast for all his servants; and he lifted up the head of the chief cupbearer and the head of the chief baker among his servants. 21 He restored the chief cupbearer to his office, and he put the cup into Pharaoh's hand; 22 but he hanged the chief

baker, just as Joseph had interpreted to them. [23]
Yet the chief cupbearer did not remember
Joseph, but forgot him *(emphasis added).*

Once again, Joseph is faithfully following God's will, yet it feels like his efforts yield no results for himself. He supports everyone else, but he remains in his own struggle. Have you ever felt this way? Perhaps you've prayed for someone and witnessed their healing or financial breakthrough, yet when you're the one facing sickness or desperately needing a miracle in your finances, it feels as though no one is home in heaven. You feel like you've been "Unfriended" by God or put on "Call Block."

As I mentioned earlier, my wife, Rhea, and I had been serving on staff at a church in Tennessee that we affectionately called Camelot. Everything seemed perfect. Rhea was actively involved in the worship ministry, while I focused on youth ministry, and both of our roles felt blessed by the Lord. The church was growing, the staff got along well, and the pastors felt more like family than just leaders to us. They hold a special place in our hearts, and my kids still call them Papaw and Nan, reveling in the love and attention they provide. Financially, we faced little pressure. My wife, being a preacher's kid, had spent most of her life living in church parsonages. A generous builder from the church even constructed a beautiful three-story dream home for us at cost. We felt celebrated, fulfilled, and loved. At that time, our daughter was young, and we had a baby boy on the way. That's when God came knocking and spoiled everything.

I could have stayed and been perfectly happy. However, as people who have dedicated their life to saying "Yes" to whatever the Lord asks, we chose to pack everything up and move to Texas. The vision was to plant a church there, and my wife and kids faithfully joined me on this new adventure. God had called us, and we answered. But I had high expectations! I believed that our 5,200 sq ft house would sell quickly, allowing us to use the equity we had to purchase an even better house in Texas. I thought we would start this church, and that people would flock to it. No one in town had ever approached things the way I planned to, so I envisioned the church booming and everything being wonderful.

Things started to get complicated. We moved back to the town where I grew up. My old church had an opening, and we decided to join the effort to revitalize this struggling congregation. We relocated to Texas and settled into a 1,600 sq. ft. parsonage. The garage was filled from floor to ceiling with our belongings. My wife and I continued to face challenges; we couldn't afford the house we owned in Tennessee on the salary we were earning in Texas. When the housing bubble burst, we found there were no buyers. For years, we struggled along like this.

We rented the Tennessee house to a couple who had lost their home, but they couldn't pay enough to cover the mortgage, insurance, or taxes. As a result, I had to cover about half of those costs myself. I did it because God told me to. But when I asked for relief, it seemed that God had nothing to say.

After about six years, our renters moved out, and we rented the home to a pastor. Unfortunately, after just a month, he left with almost no notice. We decided to put the house back on the market and tried to sell it at cost, as we just wanted to get out from under it. However, nothing ever came to fruition.

Finally, after seven years since leaving Tennessee, it seemed we had a potential new renter: an older couple who could pay upfront. This offered us a chance to relieve ourselves of the financial burden that had been getting tighter over time. We were behind on two payments for the house. With their deposit and the first month's rent, along with some of our own money, we could finally catch up. That's when the bank decided to foreclose. The loan officer argued with the Vice President about our situation, but he wouldn't relent. Strangely, he was unwilling to make any concessions, even though we had potential renters who were customers of that bank! It was a gut punch.

The foreclosure occurred around the same time that we had obediently left our denomination, following God's instruction. The entire church membership left with us, but we had to leave the church building and parsonage behind as we essentially started over. We had uprooted our happy family from Tennessee because we felt called by the Lord to do so. We rented our home out in an effort to lift judgment off of others, and we departed from the denomination at His leading. And yet, this is how we were rewarded for our obedience? It felt unbelievable. Needless to say, it had been a challenging seven years. Nothing went as I had anticipated.

From the very beginning, I had a dream that I believed God had placed in my heart. When He called me to preach, He was clear and specific about the scope of the ministry

I would be part of. Until we moved to Texas, everything seemed to be moving in the right direction. Every step we took felt like progress, and it appeared that the dream God had given me was finally coming to life.

But then we arrived in Texas, and it felt like we hit a wall—a buzz saw of opposition and hardship. We were vilified by many and rejected by those we thought would stand with us. Even our relationships with extended family fell apart. Financial struggles compounded the strain, and the weight of it all began to take a toll on our marriage.

The church, which had once been thriving, started to shrink. As we transitioned to being a mobile church, having to set up and tear down for each service, we could feel the momentum slipping away. It seemed like God had dropped us into a wilderness to die.

Meanwhile, friends within ministry, who we admired, were seeing their churches grow and make an impact, while we felt overlooked and forgotten. They would take our ideas—things we had poured our hearts into—and implement them with great success. Yet the same seeds, when planted in the soil we were in, withered and died. It was as if we were rejects, the ones left behind. The lie that we were forgotten was easy to hear, and in the midst of our struggles, it became even easier to believe.

The Lie: *No Good Deed Goes Unpunished*

How many times in your life have you felt this way? You were satisfied doing what you were doing, and then God came along and led you to leave a job, a church, or a city. You followed Him only to be met with one disappointment after another. In the middle of your walk of obedience, it seems that God has left you, and you are going under. Most of the time, this is when people give up and go back. They don't push through. They decide that it's over because they don't recognize that they are in the middle of their faith journey. I've been there. So have our beloved heroes talked about in the Bible. Consider Peter.

In the first chapter of Mark, the disciples regularly witnessed Jesus performing miracle after miracle for all the world to see. In Mark 1:45, it says, "But He went out and began to proclaim it freely and to spread the news around, to such an extent that Jesus could no longer publicly enter a city but stayed out in the unpopulated areas; and **they were coming to Him from everywhere**." With such an incredible ministry launch, their hopes and expectations have to be high. Super-duper high. Did I say, "HIGH?!" But then comes the betrayal, the trial, and the death of their Messiah.

For all the victories Peter has witnessed, when his faith is tested, he comes close to giving in and going back to his prior life. And he nearly takes all of the disciples with him. John 21:3 reads, "Simon Peter said to them, 'I am going fishing.' They said to him, 'We will also come with you.' They went out and got into the boat, and that night, they caught nothing."

When God seemingly hasn't come through, and we face overwhelming disappointment, our default mode is to go back to what we knew before beginning our journey of faith. In Peter's case, it's fishing. What he doesn't realize is that he is STILL LEADING, causing the other disciples to return to their default setting, as well. We must be careful to remember that others may be following us, and our decisions can impact them. The problem with any of us going back to what we used to be or do is that Jesus has ruined us for those things. They are dead to us, and we are dead to them. We aren't the sinners we used to be. Because we know the truth, we can't even enjoy sin.

These professional fishermen who used to own boats and had servants working for them, who knew the Sea of Galilee like the back of their hand, who knew where to go and what to do on the water...catch nothing all night. Yeah...you can't go back. Jesus has already turned you into a fisher of men! Just like the disciples, He has changed our identity, and our default setting to return to the former things will only bring misery, not relief. When the disciples discover Jesus on the shore waiting for them, guess what He's cooking. You got it—fish! If they had just held out a little longer...He would have provided what they needed.

Remember that no matter what it looks or feels like, it's always better to stay the course with Jesus. He will get you where you need to go. But I must confess, I get it. I wanted to give up, too. I missed our Camelot. It wasn't just how hard life had become, but how long we had to endure the hardship that had us browbeaten. Most people can endure for a season, but like the disciples, we grow weary, our eyelids get tired, and we just long for a season of rest.

As a minister or a friend, how often have you loved and supported others, only to have them turn against you? How many times have you counseled friends, family members, or church members who were experiencing crises such as marital issues, addiction, struggles with rebellious teenagers, or dealing with grief and heartache, only to see them walk away once their situation improved? It's easy to fall into the trap of feeling forgotten, believing the lie that no good deed goes unpunished. When we last left Joseph, he had interpreted the dreams of his fellow inmates and asked the chief cupbearer to remember him. He faithfully delivered the unfortunate news of the baker's untimely surmise and the soon-coming restoration of the cupbearer. He was faithful to deliver the message of God with integrity, no matter the consequences. One would think that upon the fulfillment of such a word, the cupbearer would remember him with reverence and fear. Unfortunately, the cupbearer instead chooses to have selective amnesia for a full two years. That is, until remembering Joseph can benefit his own life once again. Swindoll offers this insight[17]:

> *Those two full years for Joseph were neither exciting nor eventful. They represented a long, dull, monotonous, unspectacular, slow-moving grind. Month after month after month of . . . well, nothing. Not even the Genesis account attempts to make those years seem meaningful. Because they weren't. That's what it's like when you're in a period of waiting. Nothing's happening! Wait. Wait. Wait. Wait. On the other hand, it only seems like nothing is happening. In reality, a whole lot is happening. Events are occurring apart from our involvement. Furthermore, we are being strengthened. We are being established. We are being perfected. We are being refined.*

Refined into pure gold. We're back to my earlier comment—he's being shaped for greatness. All whom God uses greatly are first hidden in the secret of His presence, away from the pride of man. It is there our vision clears. It is there the silt drops from the current of our life and our faith begins to grasp His arm. Abraham waited for the birth of Isaac. Moses didn't lead the Exodus until he was eighty. Elijah waited beside the brook. Noah waited 120 years for rain. Paul was hidden away for three years in Arabia. The list doesn't end. God is working while His people are waiting, waiting, waiting. Joseph is being shaped for a significant future. That's what's happening. For the present time, nothing. For the future, everything!

After those two full years, Joseph experienced a turning point in his life—on a day that seemed like any other day. That morning dawned like every other morning over the previous two years. Just like the morning that dawned before Moses saw the burning bush. Just like the morning that dawned before David was anointed by Samuel as the king-elect. For Joseph, just another dungeon day—except for one little matter Joseph knew nothing about: The night before Pharaoh had a bad dream.

The Truth: *Your Reward Can't be Taken from You*

Joseph poses a key question in Genesis 40:8: "Do not interpretations belong to God?" Perhaps the dilemma we face isn't with the dream God gives us or even His execution of it; perhaps, it's with our interpretation. Most of our frustration is with things not going as we assumed. Everyone wants a fairy tale, but the problem with that is that fairy tales are fiction.

Joseph has a couple of dreams. He and his family all interpret those dreams to mean that Joseph will be so exalted that he will be lord over his family, and they will be ruled by him. God doesn't say this is going to happen. After thirteen years of slavery and prison, Joseph realizes that the interpretation of the dream comes from God alone.

We aren't qualified to interpret dreams. We can only relay the interpretation that God gives us. When we assume how the dream or promise of God will play out, we are setting ourselves up for disappointment. He doesn't do things our way. Our way doesn't really have a chance. In his own words, He says:

Isaiah 55:8-9 (NASB)
8 *"For My thoughts are not your thoughts, nor are your ways My ways," declares the Lord.* 9 *"For as the heavens are higher than the earth, so are My ways higher than your ways and My thoughts than your thoughts.*

In Joseph's case, his reward cannot be power, authority, or position. He has been stripped of his comfort and status as the favorite son, lost his authority in Potiphar's house, and, being confined to prison, seems to have no opportunity for power. Therefore, his reward must be something greater and unassailable. Otherwise, he would have long ago slipped into depression and bitterness. His true reward is the knowledge that his Heavenly Father is pleased with him.

> If we pursue what cannot be taken from us, we will never lose what we desire most.

In all that Joseph does, regardless of his circumstances, he seeks to please his Heavenly Father. Throughout all his years of testing, Joseph's faithfulness never wavers. His living conditions change repeatedly; he moves in and out of favor with others, and his circumstances range from the pit to slavery to prison. Yet no matter the upheaval around him, he remains focused on God. As a result, his reward is a pleased Father. The Heavenly Father is our ultimate reward, and that is a gift no one can take from us. Let this truth sink in deeply: if we pursue what cannot be taken from us, we will never lose what we desire most.

The Fruit: *Him*

I remember the moment like it was yesterday. I was away at a ministry event when my wife called me. A certified letter from the bank had come in the mail informing us that our house in Tennessee had been foreclosed on. Unfortunately, she was the one to receive the letter and open it. She was angry...understandably so. I tried my best to comfort her, but it was to no avail. We hung up, and I asked God to help her...to help us. Neither of us could understand why He would allow this to happen to us after all that we had been through.

Unbeknownst to me, Rhea went to the Lord in prayer after we got off the phone. She has always been faithful in prayer. God spoke to her, asking her to make a little altar out of our ottoman in the living room. At His urging, she went and got a couple of items from the kitchen, laying them alongside the letter on that ottoman. She took the bread and the grape juice, surrendering herself to partaking of the Lord's table. In that moment, she remembered our Lord and handed Him that house. I wouldn't know about this for some time.

When I returned from my trip several days later, she and I had a very lively discussion. People had left the church, finances were tight, and we were truly hanging onto life by our fingernails. Now, we were losing the home we had hoped to sell in order to have money to secure a down payment for the house we were leasing. As it turned out, not only would we not have a down payment, but our credit would be destroyed. "Why would God let this happen," I wondered? "Doesn't He love us? Haven't we been faithful? What else did He want...blood?"

My beautiful bride and I were both hurting deeply, trying to grapple with it all. Despite my despair, something rose up in me in that moment and I heard myself say, "We have done everything He has asked us to do, and He has promised us that He would take care of us. Now, it is on Him. I will put my trust in nothing less than Jesus Christ. And they that put their trust in the Lord will never be put to shame!"

We instantly seemed to know that we had drawn a spiritual line in the sand. We were going to trust God, and He was either going to come through or we were going under. We were all in. We prayed together before Rhea had to leave for a ministry trip. One night, while she was gone, and our children were asleep, I had a long talk with God. I was still unaware of Rhea's act of faithful surrender on the day that she had received the certified letter. As I prayed, God told me to make an altar out of the ottoman and put the letter on it.

I'll never forget what He said. It was as clear as if someone were talking in my ear. He said,

> *"Let me tell you something, son. That house doesn't love you. I love you. That house hasn't been moved one bit concerning what you and Rhea have been through this last year. Only I have seen your tears and heard your cry. And yet you continue to look to that house to secure your tomorrows. You two have made it into an idol. It is a thing shaped with human hands. I am the one who holds your tomorrows. So, TEAR DOWN THE HIGH PLACE!"*

It is a terrible thing to discover that you are an idolater. Sadly, though, it was true. Let me fast forward for a moment in Joseph's story. In Genesis 45:5, Joseph says,

"Now do not be grieved or angry with yourselves, because you sold me here, for God sent me before you to preserve life." The root word for "grieved" means to carve, fabricate, or fashion. In essence, idols are things we fashion or shape, which then shape us. In the middle of our story, I had not yet fully assimilated what Joseph came to know in the middle of his story. God wasn't trying to take something from my family...He was giving us something.

Instead of trusting God, we had trusted in that house to secure our future, protect us, and provide for us. God wanted to know if He was enough for me. Did I trust Him? I decided He is enough, and that I will continually trust Him. A monumental shift occurred as He became my one desire. The house no longer mattered, and I stopped asking Him to save it. As I sacrificed it to the Lord that day, He reminded me of something I had recently learned. The priest of the Lord has no inheritance but the Lord.

Deuteronomy 18:1-2 (NASB)
1 "The Levitical priests, the whole tribe of Levi, shall have no portion or inheritance with Israel; they shall eat the Lord's offerings by fire and His portion. 2 They shall have no inheritance among their countrymen; the Lord is their inheritance, as He promised them.

Come what may, it was time to trust Him fully. No more idols. I just wanted Him. The Lord is inheritance enough. He is my portion, and He is more than enough.

When I got up off of my knees, we still needed a miracle. The house aside, we needed help with bills. I felt God's assurance that He would give us the breakthrough we needed. In faith, I asked God for $10,000. It would pay everything, allow us to get the house out of foreclosure, and put some money in savings.

When Rhea returned home, I told her about my request to the Lord. Immediately, the phone rang. A lawyer called, wanting to purchase the rights to something I owned on the internet. I still don't know how in the world he obtained my number. I have signed a non-disclosure agreement, so I can't tell you the details, but suffice it to say, we received a nice sum of money. It allowed us to pay some bills and take the edge off, even though we were not completely out of the woods yet.

A week later, I preached a funeral for someone I had never met. The family was devastated by this young woman's sudden death, and I helped guide them through each step. After the funeral, they handed me a "Thank You" card. When I got to my truck and opened it, I had to look twice. It contained $2000. Rhea and I decided to give half of it as an offering.

> What we do with money reveals our
> hearts, desires, and our motives.

I want to point out that the Bible contains over 500 verses about prayer and about 500 verses on faith. That seems like a lot until you realize it has more than 2,000 verses on money and possessions. Of Jesus' parables, sixteen out of thirty-eight are about money. What we do with money reveals our hearts, desires, and our motives.

Rhea and I have always believed that being faithful givers is as important as paying our bills. At this point, we were caught up on everything except the house. The date of foreclosure, February 13th, came and went. Ten days later, we were streaming a revival at a church pastored by a friend of mine. I sat watching it in total silence with no apparent facial expression. My wife couldn't read me. She wondered if I was skeptical of what we were seeing. She asked me what I was thinking. I told her I felt I was supposed to be there the next night. It was out of state, so I would need to take our last $400 and buy a plane ticket to fly halfway across the country, rent a car, and drive three hours to the revival. I would have to return immediately for a church event, meaning I would fly there and back in less than twenty-four hours. Rhea prayed and agreed. So, I bought my ticket. I texted the pastor that I was coming to see him tomorrow. He texted back, "Did you get my letter?" I didn't know what he was talking about. He asked me again. Again, I told him I didn't know what he was talking about. He asked, "What are you doing?" I said, "God has told me to come fly to your service tomorrow night." He couldn't believe it. He told me that when Rhea received the letter the next day, she needed to wait to read it until he could talk to me. Puzzled, I agreed.

The next day, my bride received another certified letter. Again, alone and without me. She sat down on the ottoman and opened it up. I was in Tennessee, and God rocked me that night when I sat in the front row. God spoke through the speaker, saying, "For you man of God, it's not how hard the battle has been, but it's how long it's lasted...". There is more, but it's not for this book. I was in tears as God ministered to me that night, breathing life into me.

Afterward, the pastor invited me back to the green room, and as we sat down, he told me a story. He had gone to speak at a prayer conference. Ice hit the metroplex, and the service was cancelled. He was staying with a friend of his, who my wife and I had never met, who, for some weird reason, asked about Rhea and me. He wanted to know what had happened when we left the denomination. My friend relayed the story, and his friend, moved with compassion, told him that he wanted to write each of us a check. He asked if my friend would overnight them to us. He agreed. I said, "Wait a minute. When was this?" He told me it was Feb 10th.

Just then, Rhea called my phone, screaming with excitement. In her hands was more than double the miracle I had asked God for. I said, "I thought he told you to overnight it." This would have gotten the money to us the day before the foreclosure. He apologized and said that he had forgotten to do that and had been carrying the checks around in his coat pocket for a couple of weeks!

I asked him if he knew what I would have done if he had sent that to me on time. Even though he didn't know anything about the house, he prophetically replied, "Sink it into a dead idol?" And there it was. God's divine delay was working in my favor. I totaled up all that I had spent out of pocket on that house over the course of the seven-year struggle. It equaled $1000 LESS than what God had given me in two weeks! It is also important to note that we received double what I would have netted had we sold the house at our top asking price.

The priest of the Lord has no inheritance. The Lord is his inheritance. I didn't need that house at all. I needed Him. God is so good. He gave my wife another certified letter moment. He took care of us as He promised, and instead of giving me $10,000, we were able to secure our home, and then, we gave $10,000 away!

The fruit of pressing through neglect and being forgotten is receiving Him. He is all we need. He should be our all-consuming desire. Desire and passion for God are foundational to understanding Joseph's relationship with the Father. It is not a religious relationship. If it were, it would be too weak to withstand all he has to endure. In "Surprised by the Power of the Spirit", Jack Deere writes[18]:

> *"I had embraced a form of Christianity that radically separated obedience and feelings. Obedience without emotion is nothing more than discipline or will power. It is not love. You cannot take the passion out of love and still have love. True love manifests itself not only in acts but also in feelings. Affection and passion are indispensable aspects of love for God. The goal of the Christian life is not simply external obedience to the written commands of God. The goal of Christian life is to obey God from the heart (Rom. 6:17; Eph. 6:6). No one can obey God from the heart unless the commands of God are written on his heart. This is the great difference between the Old Testament saint and New Testament believer. Because we have access to the ministry of the*

Holy Spirit, He writes the commands of God on our hearts (Jer. 31:33; Heb. 10:16). We do not have to be content with external obedience. We can hate what God hates and love what God loves.

I was defending a system that actually justified lukewarm feelings toward God and His children. Yet Jesus said to the Laodiceans, "So, because you are lukewarm - neither hot nor cold - I am about to spit you out of my mouth" (Rev. 3:16). In 1746 Jonathan Edwards published a book, The Religious Affections, in which he argued that "True religion must consist very much in the affections.'"

Perhaps this is one reason so many Christians wither in the heat of trial. They lack the depth of relationship and passion for God necessary to withstand the tribulations that come in this life. Head knowledge will not be enough to sustain you in the middle of neglect. Moreover, don't discount the value of the work God wants to do in you. Steve Uppal speaks to the value of dying to self and its reward[19]:

"True biblical Christianity really begins through death which then leads to life. The problem for many today is that we are trying to access the life and power of God without embracing death. This leads to frustration and weakness in believers who end up

living powerless lives, constantly struggling to overcome. It is also the reason we have so many weak, man-made churches which are void of the power of God. The power of the Holy Spirit flows through those who have died and now live to the Spirit. The words from a greeting card express this well:

All of self, none of GodLess of self, more of GodNone of self, all of God.

We must die to our own expectations and subscribe to the hope of His plan. And hope in Him is one that doesn't disappoint. My interpretation of how God's promise would play out was completely wrong. Joseph's dreams are no different. It isn't about him ruling his family. It's about him being positioned to make a way for them. More on that later.

What are you holding onto? What are you trusting in that you believe will secure your tomorrow? What idols are shaping you? Let them all go. Tear down the high places in your life. Be released from your desire to be awesome. Realize that God is more than enough, His timing is better than yours, and His plan is so much greater. Cultivate a passionate relationship with your Heavenly Father, and don't give up in the middle of neglect.

CHAPTER 7

In the Middle of Fulfillment

Delays are only learning experiences to help you focus more aptly on the journey.

"If God delays us, it is only to get our eyes off ourselves and back on Him and His promise. Satan, however, strives to detour us from reaching our goals. He sidetracks us with selfish interests so that we lose our way. Detours—things that deter your focus and defer your interest—may change your entire course or direction. Delays are only learning experiences to help you focus more aptly on the journey. The difference between a detour and a delay is simple: when the direction in which you are moving takes you away from your desired goal, it's a detour; when

it complements and corresponds with your
destination, then it is simply a delay."[20]

I T'S THAT SIMPLE. IT's that hard. To fully trust God is to
also declare that we are unqualified to know the future,
what it needs, and how to navigate it. What may seem to
be a detour, such as a prison, may actually be a Divine
delay. Time and space are not just for the astrophysicist
to comprehend. We, as children of the Most High God,
must come to grapple with the eternal truth that God is
timeless and outside of space and yet works like a virtuoso
within time and space, especially *our* time and *our* space.
Again, we aren't qualified to navigate the dream or the
future. We must trust Him. He is working in a manner that
we cannot, at times, see or comprehend. Joseph's path
isn't made evident by the two dreams he has at seventeen
years of age. They *seem* to be about power, authority, and
position.

The steps to those things in the kingdom of men are
upward and onward. God's trajectory that He plots for
Joseph, however, is down and dirty. Who would've guessed
the steps would be from the pit to the prison and then
into the palace? That doesn't make sense to us. Yet, it is
exactly what happens. Os Hillman writes in *The Joseph
Calling* about how he had experienced this paradox. He
offers what he discovered about the transformative power
of trial[21]:

> *"God was turning my mess into messages*
> *and me into a messenger. God often puts*
> *us through the experience and discipline of*

darkness to teach us to hear and obey him. We can then become his messengers as he births a message through our oftentimes painful life experiences."

The Problem: *Getting Everything You Ever Dreamed Of*

Finally, at long last, Joseph is remembered because the king has a dream, and no one can interpret it. They send for the prisoner who so expertly interpreted the dreams of Pharaoh's servants two years earlier. Joseph is showered, shaved, and dressed to come before the ruler of the land. He listens to Pharaoh's dreams about seven fat cows and seven skinny cows, and then he relays what God reveals to him.

> **Genesis 41:25-49 (NASB)**
> *25 Now Joseph said to Pharaoh, "Pharaoh's dreams are one and the same; God has told to Pharaoh what He is about to do. 26 The seven good cows are seven years; and the seven good ears are seven years; the dreams are one and the same. 27 The seven lean and ugly cows that came up after them are seven years, and the seven thin ears scorched by the east wind will be seven years of famine. 28 It is as I have spoken to Pharaoh: God has shown to Pharaoh what He is about to do. 29 Behold, seven years of great abundance*

are coming in all the land of Egypt; ³⁰ *and after them seven years of famine will come, and all the abundance will be forgotten in the land of Egypt, and the famine will ravage the land.* ³¹ *So the abundance will be unknown in the land because of that subsequent famine; for it will be very severe.* ³² *Now as for the repeating of the dream to Pharaoh twice, it means that the matter is determined by God, and God will quickly bring it about.* ³³ *Now let Pharaoh look for a man discerning and wise, and set him over the land of Egypt.* ³⁴ *Let Pharaoh take action to appoint overseers in charge of the land, and let him exact a fifth of the produce of the land of Egypt in the seven years of abundance.* ³⁵ *Then let them gather all the food of these good years that are coming, and store up the grain for food in the cities under Pharaoh's authority, and let them guard it.* ³⁶ *Let the food become as a reserve for the land for the seven years of famine which will occur in the land of Egypt, so that the land will not perish during the famine."* ³⁷ *Now the proposal seemed good to Pharaoh and to all his servants.* ³⁸ ***Then Pharaoh said to his servants, "Can we find a man like this, in whom is a divine spirit?"*** ³⁹ ***So Pharaoh said to Joseph, "Since God has informed you of all this, there is no one so discerning and wise as you are.*** ⁴⁰ ***You shall be over my house, and according*** *to your command all my people shall do homage; only in the throne I will be greater than you." [41] Pharaoh said to Joseph, "See, I have set you over all the land of Egypt." [42] Then Pharaoh took off his signet ring from his hand and put it on Joseph's hand, and clothed him in garments of fine linen and put the gold necklace around his neck. [43] He had him ride in his second chariot; and they proclaimed before him, "Bow the knee!" And he set him over all the land of Egypt. [44] Moreover, Pharaoh said to Joseph, "Though I am Pharaoh, yet without your permission no one shall raise his hand or foot in all the land of Egypt." [45] Then Pharaoh named Joseph Zaphenath-paneah; and he gave him Asenath, the daughter of Potiphera priest of On, as his wife. And Joseph went forth over the land of Egypt.* [46] Now Joseph was thirty years old when he stood before Pharaoh, king of Egypt. And Joseph went out from the presence of Pharaoh and went through all the land of Egypt. [47] During the seven years of plenty the land brought forth abundantly. [48] So he gathered all the food of these seven years which occurred in the land of Egypt and placed the food in the cities; he placed in every city the food from its own surrounding fields. [49] Thus Joseph stored up grain in great abundance like the sand of the

sea, until he stopped measuring it, for it was
beyond measure (emphasis added).

Sometimes, having your dreams come true presents new dilemmas. They come with their own snares. Joseph is given position, authority, and power like few have ever experienced in the history of the world. As the old saying goes, "Absolute power corrupts absolutely." What is the difference with Joseph? What do you think would have happened if he, at seventeen, had been given these things shortly after having the dreams? He could have used his power to lord it over his brothers. He could have used his position for every carnal whim. He might have taken advantage of his authority and used it vindictively. However, Joseph does none of these things. Why? Because he has matured to a place of being able to handle authority correctly. He has submitted to God while being put THROUGH the process of being made into a great leader, and his willingness to yield and be cut on has made the difference between him *responding to* versus *reacting to* his brothers' hardship. Think about it. There are clues to this in the first part of his encounter with Pharaoh. Charles Swindoll puts it this way[22]:

> *He said, in effect, "Pharaoh, there's a God up*
> *there behind those stars that your soothsayers*
> *are always gazing at but have no relationship*
> *with. And I'm here to tell you, He and He*
> *alone is the One who handles dreams." When*
> *that happens, he says, literally, "God will give*
> *Pharaoh peace." Isn't that great? "Pharaoh,*

God will bring shalom to you. He will give a peaceful answer. And if it's from God, it'll be right." You know why Joseph could be so humble and speak so openly? Because his heart had been broken. Because he had been tried by the fire of affliction. Because while his external circumstances seemed almost unbearable during those years, his internal condition had been turned into pure gold. We are now witnessing the benefits of enduring affliction with one's eyes on God. Throughout the rest of Joseph's life, from age 30 to age 110 when he died, we will hear not one word of resentment on his heart or from his lips. Not a word of blame against the brothers who sold him into slavery, not a word of bitterness against Potiphar's wife, not a word of rebuke against the cupbearer who had forgotten him. Joseph was eventually in a position to get even with all of them. But he didn't...

A number of years ago, somebody counted the promises in the Bible and totaled up 7,474. I can't verify that number, but I do know that within the pages of the Bible there are thousands of promises that grab the reader and say, "Believe me! Accept me! Hold on to me!" And of all the promises in the Bible, the ones that often mean the most are the promises that offer hope at the end of affliction. Those promises that tell us, "It's worth it.

Walk with Me. Trust Me. Wait with Me. I
will reward you for that waiting time. Your
gold is being refined." Joseph learned that a
broken and contrite heart is not the end, but the
beginning. Bruised and crushed by the blows
of disappointment and unrealized dreams, he
discovered that God had never left his side.
When the affliction ended, he had been refined
and he came forth as gold. He had become a
person of greater stability, of deeper quality, of
profound character. God's promises are just as
much for us as they were for Joseph. His grace
is still at work. His tender mercies accompany
us from the pit to the pinnacle.

The Lie: *God Helps Those Who Help Themselves*

We want to resist pain, heartache, and difficulty. Our flesh longs for comfort. But nobody ever became strong through comfort, especially in today's culture. We are taught to look out for ourselves, look into our hearts, take care of ourselves, fight for ourselves, and take the bull by the horns. We live among people who celebrate those who take charge and view those who take over as courageous. Roxanne Brant warns us[23]:

> *"We must not presume to go ahead of the Lord*
> *and do what He has not required us to do.*
> *Neither should we rebel against the Lord and*

go our own separate ways. We are to follow Him and walk with Him. To presume upon Him and walk ahead of Him is as bad a sin as to rebel against Him and go our own separate ways."

Waiting for God, not getting ahead of Him, and submitting to His crazy plan is what takes real courage. We feel better just to be moving. We are not accustomed to waiting. We are such a microwave, cell phone pinging, livestream streaming, instant...everything culture.

I remember standing with a group of people one time at a restaurant. We were waiting to be seated and were told the wait might be forty-five minutes. Some of the group members didn't want to wait that long. One lady said she called another restaurant across town and there was no waiting.

I pointed out that getting across town would take twenty-five minutes. Getting this large group into the cars would take five minutes, and once we arrived, they would need to get the tables together because they didn't take reservations over the phone. So, by the time we got there and sat down, it would be close to the same time as the wait we were currently enduring. Plus, the wait time of forty-five minutes was only an approximation.

I convinced half of the people. The other half left (irritated at me, by the way). Not only did we sit down before them and finish eating before they did, but we were closer to home than where they had driven in hopes of saving time. They felt better being in control and moving, but it actually wasn't the best plan. Patience and fellowship were the better way. But they were, and still are, control freaks.

> Time is a tool God uses to shape us and transform us.

How often do we do that with God's plan? We take over because things are taking too long, and we feel better doing...something...anything other than just standing around...waiting. This is even more true when pain is part of the ordeal. We want to avoid it at all costs. The enemy wants nothing more than for YOU to be in control. Because if you are the captain of your own soul, then you are doomed. My grandmother used to sing a song that said, "Give up and let Jesus take over!" If only.

The Truth: *God's Work Starts IN You*

We don't want to go through these terrible times, but that is exactly what we need: time. Time is a tool God uses to shape us and transform us.

> *At age thirty, Joseph could never have handled this world-class task without an intensive and experience-oriented course in management. It began in Potiphar's house, where he managed all of his affairs. It continued in prison where he was eventually responsible for all the prisoners. And thirteen years later, he was "put . . . in charge of the whole land of Egypt" (41:41). God's plan for Joseph was on*

schedule. His preparation was tailor-made for the task God had for him. And because Joseph passed each test, learned from each experience, and learned to trust God more, he was ready when God opened the door of opportunity. He handled prestige and power without succumbing to pride. He persevered with patience and performed his duties faithfully and successfully. He was well prepared.[24]

God also uses space. Where He sent you, that thing you went through—the trials are part of His shaping. He uses time and space to put in you the necessary strength and integrity to wield for His purposes, that which He blesses you with later. One of my favorite authors is a man I consider a modern-day Paul in spirit. He is gifted in seeing into the Word and explaining it in a way that is revelatory. Jack Hayford writes something about supplication that deals with time and even pain[25]:

"Supplication may at first seem to be no more than praying in the will of God or "asking according to His will" or "interceding to the intent that what boundaries He intended from the beginning be reestablished." But there is an essential difference. It is time. Supplication is (1) a continually praying – an ongoing quest for a given matter to be settled in God's will and, (2) it is also a contingent praying – a quest for God's order in God's timing.

Both involve time: the first, by the passage of time during continued prayer. This is not so much to focus on the duration of any one given season of prayer, but to emphasize the consistent bearing up of the matter in prayer over a period of time – as long as it takes.

The second concern is the contingency of God's timing...

Nothing happens for the blessing of mankind without a struggle. To understand that, we need to look at the cross where Jesus died. ***Not even God could redeem man or solve the infinitely complex puzzle of how the tangle of lives in sin might be unraveled without his own suffering and death.***

It took time. It took God entering the context of time. And it took supplication" (emphasis added).

What an amazing revelation! Even God had to use suffering and time to fulfill His promise to mankind. We all want God to do a work through us. But I have found that He must do a work *in* us and *to* us **before** He can do a work *through* us.

The Fruit: *Becoming a Preserver of Life*

Genesis 45:1-15;24-27 (NASB)
*[1] Then Joseph could not control himself before all those who stood by him, and he cried, "Have everyone go out from me." So there was no man with him when Joseph made himself known to his brothers. [2] He wept so loudly that the Egyptians heard it, and the household of Pharaoh heard of it. [3] Then Joseph said to his brothers, "I am Joseph! Is my father still alive?" But his brothers could not answer him, for they were dismayed at his presence. [4] Then Joseph said to his brothers, "Please come closer to me." And they came closer. And he said, "I am your brother Joseph, whom you sold into Egypt. [5] **Now do not be grieved or angry with yourselves, because you sold me here, for God sent me before you to preserve life.** [6] For the famine has been in the land these two years, and there are still five years in which there will be neither plowing nor harvesting. [7] **God sent me before you to preserve for you a remnant in the earth, and to keep you alive by a great deliverance. [8] Now, therefore, it was not you who sent me here, but God; and He has made me a father to Pharaoh and lord of all his household and ruler over all the land of Egypt. [9] Hurry***

and go up to my father, and say to him, 'Thus says your son Joseph, "God has made me lord of all Egypt; come down to me, do not delay. *10 You shall live in the land of Goshen, and you shall be near me, you and your children and your children's children and your flocks and your herds and all that you have. 11 There I will also provide for you, for there are still five years of famine to come, and you and your household and all that you have would be impoverished."' 12 Behold, your eyes see, and the eyes of my brother Benjamin see, that it is my mouth which is speaking to you. 13 Now you must tell my father of all my splendor in Egypt, and all that you have seen; and you must hurry and bring my father down here." 14 Then he fell on his brother Benjamin's neck and wept, and Benjamin wept on his neck. 15 He kissed all his brothers and wept on them, and afterward his brothers talked with him.*

24 So he sent his brothers away, and as they departed, he said to them, "Do not quarrel on the journey." 25 Then they went up from Egypt, and came to the land of Canaan to their father Jacob. 26 They told him, saying, **"Joseph is still alive, and indeed he is ruler over all the land of Egypt."** *But he was stunned, for he did not believe them. 27 When they told him all the words of Joseph that he had spoken to them, and when he saw the wagons that Joseph had* *sent to carry him,* **the spirit of their father Jacob revived** *(emphasis added).*

Here, we discover the purpose of Joseph's suffering. He doesn't try to pay his brothers back with evil. He doesn't need to retaliate. He doesn't even want to say, "I told you so." He has gained an understanding in the pit, in slavery, and in prison that he never would have had without those experiences. He is secure enough in his identity in the Heavenly Father to know how to handle power and authority once he is trusted with it. He has been the least in class as a slave and stayed in the lowest of places in the dungeon. As a result, he has compassion for others. His suffering has brought forth fruit, after all.

Joseph refuses to see himself as a victim, nor does he see himself as a victor over his brothers. He knows his place. He is meant to be a preserver of life. **ALL** his dreams have come true, but **NONE** of their purpose is for himself. He won't even have a tribe named after him. Instead, that honor will be passed on to his sons. Just as Jesus later comes to do, Joseph has gone before his brethren to make a way for them. He has been sent to the lowliest of places and dwelt among the lowliest of men in order to raise others up and save them from destruction. If Joseph had given up in the pit, given himself over to Potiphar's wife, given out in the prison, and not pressed through the middle of his story...he would have never seen the palace, much less fulfilled his true purpose. Joseph's father is revived, his family is saved, his legacy is secured, his dreams are fulfilled, and even his bones make it to the Promised Land.

What are you facing right now that has you wanting to quit? What is pressing in on you and making you want to give up? What would you abort if you gave up now? Perhaps God has sent you into this time and has you in the middle of this rejection, comparison, betrayal, bondage, or neglect in order for you to be a way-maker for others. Perhaps we all are supposed to become preservers of life. Don't give up...God isn't finished with you yet...you're just in the middle of your story.

CHAPTER 8

On the Other Side of the Middle: Legacy

W AS THE DREAM EVER really about Joseph? Is his promotion all that is at stake? Is his life the only life the dream is meant for? If we learn anything about Joseph's journey, it should be that the dream God gives him isn't really about him as much as it is about others. Joseph has gone through several stages—from dreamer to slave, to prisoner, and then to ruler. The painful process of rejection, betrayal, neglect, and finally, elevation makes him a fully formed man of God. He can finally properly interpret his own dream, as I pointed out earlier in Genesis 45:5. It isn't about him ruling over his family; it is actually about him becoming a preserver of life for his family. Now, the question is, how far does the dream reach? Does it go beyond one man and one family? What about you and your situation? What is truly at stake? Is it just about you or is there a line of people you cannot quite see yet that will be eternally impacted by what you do next? Have you allowed God to take you through this process?

The Problem: *The Dreamer Dies*

Genesis 50 (NASB)

[22] *Now Joseph stayed in Egypt, he and his father's household, and Joseph lived one hundred and ten years.* [23] *Joseph saw the third generation of Ephraim's sons; also the sons of Machir, the son of Manasseh, were born on Joseph's knees.* [24] *Joseph said to his brothers, "I am about to die, but God will surely take care of you and bring you up from this land to the land which He promised on oath to Abraham, to Isaac and to Jacob."* [25] *Then Joseph made the sons of Israel swear, saying, "God will surely take care of you, and you shall carry my bones up from here."* [26] *So Joseph died at the age of one hundred and ten years; and he was embalmed and placed in a coffin in Egypt.*

Joseph is dead now, and one could argue that the dream has died with him. Some might argue that this was all about one guy helping save his family despite themselves. Sure, some Egyptians and other people groups were affected as a result, but the dream was really about one family. But was it really? From this one family, an entire nation was born named Israel. And, from this nation, there arose priests and kings who have led the charge of faithfully following after God. What's more, is that in the fullness of time and space, out of this family, there was born a Man who has become our Great High Priest. He is the King of kings, and His name is Jesus.

In approximately thirty-three years on earth, Jesus managed to alter the entire trajectory of human history, establishing a faith in the God of Israel that was once relegated to one little family. Millennia later, billions of people have placed their faith in Jesus Christ and His ability to save them from sin, redeeming them from eternal damnation, and restoring their life to wholeness.

I would venture to say I would not be an evangelist had Joseph given up in the middle of his story. His suffering was a foreshadowing of Jesus' role as Messiah. He had to live out his destiny, so that the gospel of the Kingdom could be birthed in the earth. I would argue that what Joseph chose to do in continuing to submit to the Lord, no matter how terrible the trial was, didn't just impact him by raising him out of prison to the palace. Nor did it just save his immediate family (his parents, brothers, wives, and their children). Rather, Joseph's obedience in suffering has impacted the whole of humanity. My question is, "Have you let it impact you?" If you haven't placed your faith in Jesus Christ, now is a great time to do so. Pray with me:

God of Joseph, the dreamer, I believe You sent forth Jesus Christ in the fullness of time and space to save me from my sins, to rescue me from the famine of my soul, and to restore me to a life of wholeness. I ask You to forgive me of my sins. I repent and turn to You, seeking salvation. I believe Jesus Christ is Lord and I place my trust in Him. Please be the Lord of my life. God, please be my Heavenly Father and lead me along the best paths for my life. In Jesus' name, I ask. Amen.

Friend, if you have said that prayer for the first time, I want to be the first to welcome you to the family of God! I am your brother in Christ, and I look forward to hearing from you. Please let me know that you have chosen to make Jesus the Lord of your life. You can find my email at the back of this book. I would love to hear from you. I want to let you know that I celebrate you. Not only that, but the Bible tells us there is a party going on in heaven over you right now. Luke 15:10 says, "In the same way, I tell you, there is joy in the presence of the angels of God over one sinner who repents." I know they had a party the day I accepted Jesus!

In real-time, the fulfillment of Joseph's dream was a multi-national event. Egypt, at the time, was the most powerful, populous, and advanced society on earth. What they did as a nation impacted the nations around them. Even the biblical account shows that they sold the stored food to other non-Egyptian people. When the famine rocked on through the years, these groups began to sell land rights for food. Egypt gobbled up more territory without having to go to war. They expanded their empire bloodlessly. What Joseph did would literally rewrite the map! Sustaining his family and gaining the gratitude and favor of Pharaoh ensured that these brothers would become twelve tribes and very quickly a huge nation within a nation. But then, Joseph dies. The end. Roll Credits. Or so it seems.

The Lie: *The Dream Dies with the Dreamer*

Within his lifetime, Joseph's dream, and his obedience to God affects millions of people, saving countless lives. The real lie would be that the dream dies with the dreamer, though. What if you had a dream from God but never lived to see it? Is the dream dead? If you think so, I'd like for you to go to Disney World and tell me if Walt Disney's dream died with him. How much more, if God is in it?

> **Exodus 1 (NASB)**
> *⁶ Joseph died, and all his brothers and all that generation. ⁷ But the sons of Israel were fruitful and increased greatly, and multiplied, and became exceedingly mighty, so that the land was filled with them.*

Joseph spent so many years in seemingly unfruitful places only to give birth to prosperity and fruitfulness that would go far beyond his own life. His family would increase greatly, multiply, become exceedingly mighty, and fill the land! They became a force to be reckoned with. Even when they finally leave Egypt, Joseph's influence is still vibrant four centuries later. They fulfill his last request to take his bones with them.

Joseph died at 110—the age Egyptians considered the perfect length of a divinely blessed life—and his body was handled in the typical Egyptian way: mummification. Before he died, he made his family swear to bury him in the land of promise, which Hebrews 11:22 commends as an exemplary act of faith. As it turns out, his embalming was providential. It would be four hundred years before Israel left Egypt. But when they did, Joseph's wish was not forgotten; Moses took his remains out of Egypt when the Hebrews fled (Exod. 13:19). Israel carried them for forty years in the wilderness and buried them on Jacob's tract of land at Shechem (Josh. 24:32). Symbolically, just as Joseph's body could not be held in the land of Israel's captivity, Jesus's body could not be held in the place of our captivity—this world and the grave.[26]

> You aren't limited by YOUR limitations. You are free to walk in the favor of the LIMITLESS GOD!

Joseph's final journey would outlive a generation! His bones would outlast those who saw the Red Sea part. He would make it into the Promised Land while many would die in the wilderness. Even death couldn't keep him from traveling! The implications for us blow me away. We are too limited in what we believe that God can do. He is able to go far beyond our limits and our imagination.

What is it that you are facing? Enlarge your vision to look beyond the right now and see this massive, all-powerful, loving God who is going to keep His promises. You aren't limited by YOUR limitations. You are free to walk in the favor of the LIMITLESS GOD!

The Truth: *The Life of the Dream Depends on the Dream GIVER*

In Exodus 13:17-22, Moses carries the bones of Joseph out of Egypt and all through the wilderness. In Joshua 24:32, we read how Joseph is finally buried with his family in the Promised Land. It could be argued that the life of a dream comes to an end at the final resting place of the dreamer. However, this perspective focuses solely on the one who dreamed the dream, overlooking the Dream Giver, God Himself. There was always more to the story than Joseph, and there is another Person in your life story as well.

Our journey through experiences of comparison, rejection, betrayal, bondage, neglect, and even fulfillment guides us to focus so much on our feelings, our needs, and our circumstances that we forget about our Main Companion. When we do think of God, we often do so to blame Him for not acting as we expected. But, make no mistake, He is near. Let me show you what I mean:

> **Psalm 34 (NASB)**
> *15 The eyes of the Lord are toward the righteousAnd His ears are open to their cry.16 The face of the Lord is against evildoers, To cut off the memory of them from the earth.17 The righteous cry, and the Lord hearsAnd delivers them out of all their troubles.18 The Lord is near to the brokenheartedAnd saves those who are crushed in spirit.*

¹⁹ Many are the afflictions of the righteous, But the Lord delivers him out of them all.²⁰ He keeps all his bones, Not one of them is broken.²¹ Evil shall slay the wicked, And those who hate the righteous will be condemned.²² The Lord redeems the soul of His servants, And none of those who take refuge in Him will be condemned.

Proverbs 5:21 (NKJV)
For the ways of man are before the eyes of the LORD, and He ponders all his paths.

God is near. He sees you. He cares about you. He is especially near to the brokenhearted, and all that you have walked through. God is thoughtfully considering everything, preparing not only the fulfillment of your dreams but also the hopes and futures of your children and countless others—you may be unable to fully grasp the magnitude of it all. What if your current struggles are about something far greater than just this moment? What if they extend to influence nations and ripple through a thousand moments, some reaching far beyond your own lifetime? What if you are a way maker...a preserver of life? The dream or promise isn't just dependent on the dreamer...it primarily depends on the Dream Giver...the Promise Maker! And HE has no end!

The Fruit: *The Dream Endures Far Beyond the Dreamer*

Joseph is reminisced about in the Bible over and over again. People have sung about him, talked about him, and found strength and encouragement from his story. His life became prophetic in that it foretold the sufferings and ultimate victory of Christ. His namesake would be chosen for the earthly father of Jesus. Oh, how the dream endured far beyond the dreamer! Even the psalmist sang of the redemptive story of this man:

> **Psalm 105 (NASB)**
> *[16] And He called for a famine upon the land; He broke the whole staff of bread. [17] He sent a man before them, Joseph, who was sold as a slave. [18] They afflicted his feet with fetters, He himself was laid in irons; [19] Until the time that his word came to pass, The word of the Lord tested him. [20] The king sent and released him, The ruler of peoples, and set him free. [21] He made him lord of his house And ruler over all his possessions, [22] To imprison his princes at will, That he might teach his elders wisdom. [23] Israel also came into Egypt; Thus Jacob sojourned in the land of Ham. [24] And He caused His people to be very fruitful, And made them stronger than their adversaries.*

With the birth of the church in the New Testament, everything changes. We read how Stephen is martyred for preaching Jesus. At his execution, Stephen preaches a message that impacts the man assigned to hold the coats of the executioners that day. This man, Paul, would one day write three-fourths of the New Testament. Sure enough, this sermon about the validity of Jesus as the Messiah includes the story of Joseph.

> **Acts 7 (NASB)**
> *[9] "The patriarchs became jealous of Joseph and sold him into Egypt. Yet God was with him, [10] and rescued him from all his afflictions, and granted him favor and wisdom in the sight of Pharaoh, king of Egypt, and he made him governor over Egypt and all his household. [11] "Now a famine came over all Egypt and Canaan, and great affliction with it, and our fathers could find no food. [12] But when Jacob heard that there was grain in Egypt, he sent our fathers there the first time. [13] On the second visit Joseph made himself known to his brothers, and Joseph's family was disclosed to Pharaoh. [14] Then Joseph sent word and invited Jacob his father and all his relatives to come to him, seventy-five persons in all. [15] And Jacob went down to Egypt and there he and our fathers died."*

You may be going through a difficult time right now. You might be facing rejection, betrayal, or are feeling forgotten and neglected by those you have loved or trusted. However, when everything is said and done, those people will not be able to tell their story without including you! Think of Joseph, who could not be overlooked; he paved the way for so many that when the history of the nation is recounted, his name is a part of it. You are a preserver of life. Although you are going through hell right now, remember the words of Winston Churchill: "Keep going!"

Your life isn't over...you're just in the middle of your story.

CHAPTER 9

Epilogue

Write in the Middle

October 2019

W HEN I BEGAN AUTHORING this book, I thought that I had already been through enough troubles to last a lifetime. I had no idea of the even more gut-wrenching trials and tests that lay ahead of me during my writing journey. Every word that I have written, every encouragement I have offered, and every truth I have shared has stemmed from a season of life in which I have endured great despair and hopelessness.

I have been pastoring in this city for almost thirteen years. Thirteen is an interesting number to me as it is the length of time from Joseph's dream to when he first met Pharaoh. I have faced numerous trials in my life that led me to the point of contemplating whether it would be better for me if the Lord simply took me to heaven. I have endured many battles, experienced numerous betrayals, dealt with countless disappointments, and been overwhelmed by a profound sense of failure.

Since I intend to publish this book, I am already uncomfortable with the amount of personal information in it, but I recognize that you may connect with what I have been through and that my story might offer you hope and encouragement. I am not writing from atop a high mountain, sitting on a stack of cash without a care in the world. I am writing from the dungeon. Dark. Alone. Forgotten.

Imagine what it must have been like for Joseph to have a heart full of such a beautiful dream, only for it to turn into a nightmare. Then, after years in prison, two guys arrive with dreams that need interpretation. He could have said, "Hard pass on interpreting your dreams, guys. Dreams don't come true. Look at me. Mine certainly didn't". But of course, he doesn't. When faced with using the gift of God in a place where it may have seemed as though God had forgotten him...he once again responds with a holy "Yes". Then he does something we only witness once while reading about his life story. He pleads for himself, "Remember me".

Joseph watches as both men's dreams are fulfilled – one to a place of exaltation and one to a place of demise. But is Joseph remembered as requested? Not for another two years. Imagine how it must have felt to interpret the dreams of two men and see them fulfilled within a matter of hours while Joseph had been waiting eleven years. His ability to interpret dreams would not prove critical for another two years – the gift within him was devalued, underestimated, and unappreciated. It wasn't that it wasn't legitimate; it just hadn't been exposed to the right person at the right time.

I feel like I am living in a "forgotten" moment. I am absolutely exhausted from all the "Yes, Lord" moments over the years, and honestly, I don't know if I have two more years left in me. Yet, even as I write this, I know that God has not forgotten me; He is working, as Job noted, on the left hand where I cannot see. I trust that He will fulfill His promise to me. I believe I will stand before those He sends me to, just as He has done before. He has delivered me from the desire of wanting to be awesome. I have no pride left, no worldly ambitions. I simply want Him, and I genuinely mean this.

In the heat of this latest trial, my wife asked me, "What will you do?" In response, something from a place I had never accessed before rose up and out of my mouth. "Though he slay me...yet will I trust Him." I know I am in the middle of my story. I am determined to say "Yes" to whatever He asks of me. I take courage from those who have gone before me, including those whose dreams were not fulfilled in their lifetimes. More on that in a moment.

July 2024 – Where We Are Now

Five very eventful years have passed since I wrote the preceding chapters and the first part of this epilogue. Tears filled my eyes as I re-read the last few paragraphs just now. I had not looked at this manuscript during the intervening years, and what a powerful testimony it has become in my own life. Let me give you a bit of a "Where are they now?" update.

I was born into a little church in Ennis, TX. Five generations would be part of that church body, and it was what I always knew. My family worked as worship leaders, teachers, elders, secretaries, clerks, ushers, musicians, and just about everything else one could do in church ministry. They literally built and repaired the buildings, served the church body their whole lives, mowed the grass, directed Christmas plays, counted offerings, prayed for countless people in the altars, cast out devils, and witnessed miracles. More than once, they laid hands on dead bodies and saw the God they trusted in raise the dead back to life. They had done everything...except pastor a church.

I was the last person anyone would have picked, but as it turned out, I became the first person in my family to pastor a church. I served in every way I could in that little church in Texas, just as my family members had served. And then one day...I returned as their pastor. That story turned from one of triumph to loss...and great pain. Disillusioned and heartbroken, I left our denomination. It was terrible. I'm not going to relive all of that...but you should know...I never thought I'd return. What followed were the hardest years of my life. What happened at the church and thereafter impacted every facet of life...it took its toll on my spirit, my family, my children, my finances, my reputation, my mind...everything. In my darkest moment...I prayed to die. I had one steadfast request for over a year, "Please, God, let me die." Within those moments, I wrote this book.

One night, my wife came home after spending two weeks with her mother for her open-heart surgery and recovery. I had been avoiding reaching out to her while she was away. We talked, but she had to initiate it. The night before she returned, she asked me why I was being so aloof. I told her, "I'm just trying to survive, literally." I tend to be an un-rattled, extremely optimistic, faith-filled person and the depression I was facing was something I had never dealt with.

Recently, Rhea told me it was the first and only time I wasn't there for her. Her alarmed feelings were only confirmed when she saw me sitting at the counter. She said it was like death was hanging on me. She looked at me, and we spoke no words. On the iPad I had worship music playing in an effort to change the atmosphere. As the lyrics of Brooklyn Tabernacle's "More than Enough" began to permeate the air, my eyes became as uncapped, deep wells, and I started to weep. It quickly became an ugly, uncontrollable, lose all self-composure type of wail. For six minutes and forty-nine seconds, I sat there at the counter sobbing, my body shaking like a leaf in a violent wind.

Then came a sound at the 6:50 mark of that song that the winds of my life could not stand against. It was the sound of mass intercession. I had heard it so often growing up at the altars during church, during prayer meetings led by my Mema, and every time I was with Campus Choir while at Lee University...it was a sound from my past, that for years, I had wondered if I would ever hear it again. As my wife laid hands on me with fiery tongues of intercession pouring from her lips, I succumbed to the counter's surface to hold my limp body up. As she poured out the strength of God from within her, I heard her declare, "God is INDEED enough!"

The wellspring of life within my wife and our faithful God brought me through that night. Here she was, exhausted from having ministered and cared for her mother for two weeks, and yet her love and concern for me were so deep that the first thing she did wasn't to talk about what she had been through, but to set her heart like flint to minister to me in my pain. I thank God for my wife, for her worth is far above rubies and treasures of this earth.

The Lord brought thirteen (there's that number, again) people to my mind that I was to call, many of whom I had not talked to in years. I poured my heart out to them, enduring the humiliation of self-exposure as I shared my story. These wonderful people began praying and interceding for me. Pastors, friends from Lee University & Campus Choir days, some who I'd been a youth pastor to, and even some who knew me before I came to Christ – they began to forge an incredible, and much needed hedge of prayer and intercession around my life.

After eight years of being away, I never dreamed that God would lead me back. Yet, that is exactly what happened. Once again, I found myself in the church I had known all my life—the church where I was saved during a youth camp, where Pioneers for Christ came to our church, and where I was baptized with the Holy Ghost. It was also the first place I preached, the first church I pastored, and where I went on my first mission trip. I have now been on mission trips to seventy-two countries. That church has given me people I can't imagine living without.

Now, I am a national evangelist, my wife is the director of Campus Choir at Lee University (our alma mater) ...and I am again hearing that glorious sound of intercession – the kind that breaks up the winds of destruction, defeat, and discouragement. I heard it at the revival at Lee University last year. I have heard it everywhere Campus Choir has gone these past two semesters. And I heard it again the other night as three to four hundred students at Lee came with a hunger for God to Campus Choir's six-hour prayer meeting.

Tonight, while I was praying, a familiar tune filled the air. As "More Than Enough" began, my memory was engulfed with waves of the feelings I experienced in that season. I recalled all the loss, the pain, and the great despair that had overwhelmed me, but I also remembered the hands of friends and family that God used to pull me back from the brink. This led me to reflect on the blessings that are currently surrounding me, from the fellowship with the leaders I now engage with to the reconnection with brothers whose deep love for me has become clear in ways I never knew existed. I rejoice in the fact that my new company, Once Upon a Tape, is digitizing church tapes from the 60's, 70's, 80's, and 90's and bringing back voices of past generations...who so faithfully declared the Gospel, sung His praises, and yes...carried great sounds of deep intercession.

What I celebrate the most, though, is that my wife, who was once forgotten, is now walking through one amazing opportunity after another. Our kids, who endured terrible things at the hands of church people and whom I feared we might lose to the enemy, are thriving. Our daughter, after a season of wanting nothing to do with church, recently preached her first sermon, is pursuing a ministry major, and is deeply in love with Jesus. Our son, although still in high school, is also called to ministry, and you've never seen a street evangelist like him. He can talk to anyone about the Lord.

Recently in New York City, we sent eighty college kids out to witness to people in Times Square. While many of them weren't quite sure what to do, our son Jonathan confidently encouraged his peers, saying, "Follow me." When they returned, they shared stories about the boldness and love with which he demonstrated his faith and pointed others to Jesus.

I have labored over the question, "Did I make a mistake going there...Did I miss God?" My wife and I have both intensely prayed over those questions. All I can say is we believe God sent us. But even if it was a mistake...God is still able to conform everything to the purpose of His will, as Ephesians 1 attests. So, no matter if the middle you're walking through is thrust upon you or was created by your own mistake, God will still work everything out for the good for those who are called according to His purpose (Romans 8). That's really good news!

Everything my family and I went through - the rejection, bondage, fear, comparison, loneliness...all of it...was something I really did not know if we would survive. My family was in a storm, and within that, I was in a personal storm that I could not seem to find my way out of. But we lived out the principles from God's Word that I have laid out in this book. What I discovered is that while I am not...He *IS* more than enough. The truth is that what I discovered was my pain was not the center...but it seeks to become the center. That's the conclusion many draw while feeling stuck in the middle of a wilderness or trial.

But the truth is simple. My pain and your pain are NOT the center...GOD IS!

What about you? Are you in a place of needing prayer? You don't have to wait for someone else, or a room full of people...you can make that sound of intercession yourself. Cry out to your Heavenly Father. Please believe me when I say that He is working for your good even when you can't understand it. The question is, "Do you trust Him? Is HE enough?"

I would like to share one more thing for those who are in the middle of your story. Consider this passage:

Hebrews 11 (NASB)
1 Now faith is the assurance of things hoped for, the conviction of things not seen. 2 For by it the men of old gained approval.

3 By faith we understand that the worlds were prepared by the word of God, so that what is seen was not made out of things which are visible. 4 By faith Abel offered to God a better sacrifice than Cain, through which he obtained the testimony that he was righteous, God testifying about his gifts, and through faith, though he is dead, he still speaks. 5 By faith Enoch was taken up so that he would not see death; and he was not found because God took him up; for he obtained the witness that before his being taken up he was pleasing to God. 6 And without faith it is impossible to please Him, for he who comes to God must believe that He is and that He is a rewarder of those who seek Him. ⁷ By faith Noah, being warned by God about things not yet seen, in reverence prepared an ark for the salvation of his household, by which he condemned the world, and became an heir of the righteousness which is according to faith.

⁸ By faith Abraham, when he was called, obeyed by going out to a place which he was to receive for an inheritance; and he went out, not knowing where he was going. ⁹ By faith he lived as an alien in the land of promise, as in a foreign land, dwelling in tents with Isaac and Jacob, fellow heirs of the same promise; ¹⁰ for he was looking for the city which has foundations, whose architect and builder is God. ¹¹ By faith even Sarah herself received ability to conceive, even beyond the proper time of life, since she considered Him faithful who had promised. ¹² Therefore there was born even of one man, and him as good as dead at that, as many descendants as the stars of heaven in number, and innumerable as the sand which is by the seashore.

¹³ All these died in faith, without receiving the promises, but having seen them and having welcomed them from a distance, and having confessed that they were strangers and exiles on the earth. ¹⁴ For those who say such things make it clear that they are seeking a country of their own. ¹⁵ *And indeed if they had been thinking of that country from which they went out, they would have had opportunity to return.* ¹⁶ *But as it is, they desire a better country, that is, a heavenly one. Therefore God is not ashamed to be called their God; for He has prepared a city for them.*

¹⁷ *By faith Abraham, when he was tested, offered up Isaac, and he who had received the promises was offering up his only begotten son;* ¹⁸ *it was he to whom it was said, "In Isaac your descendants shall be called."* ¹⁹ *He considered that God is able to raise people even from the dead, from which he also received him back as a type.* ²⁰ *By faith Isaac blessed Jacob and Esau, even regarding things to come.* ²¹ *By faith Jacob, as he was dying, blessed each of the sons of Joseph, and worshiped, leaning on the top of his staff.* ²² *By faith Joseph, when he was dying, made mention of the exodus of the sons of Israel, and gave orders concerning his bones.*

²³ *By faith Moses, when he was born, was hidden for three months by his parents, because they saw he was a beautiful child; and they were not afraid of the king's edict.* ²⁴ *By faith Moses, when he had grown up, refused to be called the son of Pharaoh's daughter,* ²⁵

choosing rather to endure ill-treatment with the people of God than to enjoy the passing pleasures of sin, [26] considering the reproach of Christ greater riches than the treasures of Egypt; for he was looking to the reward. [27] By faith he left Egypt, not fearing the wrath of the king; for he endured, as seeing Him who is unseen. [28] By faith he kept the Passover and the sprinkling of the blood, so that he who destroyed the firstborn would not touch them. [29] By faith they passed through the Red Sea as though they were passing through dry land; and the Egyptians, when they attempted it, were drowned.

[30] By faith the walls of Jericho fell down after they had been encircled for seven days. [31] By faith Rahab the harlot did not perish along with those who were disobedient, after she had welcomed the spies in peace.

[32] And what more shall I say? For time will fail me if I tell of Gideon, Barak, Samson, Jephthah, of David and Samuel and the prophets, [33] who by faith conquered kingdoms, performed acts of righteousness, obtained promises, shut the mouths of lions, [34] quenched the power of fire, escaped the edge of the sword, from weakness were made strong, became mighty in war, put foreign armies to flight. [35] Women received back their dead by

resurrection; and others were tortured, not accepting their release, so that they might obtain a better resurrection; ³⁶ and others experienced mockings and scourgings, yes, also chains and imprisonment. ³⁷ They were stoned, they were sawn in two, they were tempted, they were put to death with the sword; they went about in sheepskins, in goatskins, being destitute, afflicted, ill-treated ³⁸ (men of whom the world was not worthy), wandering in deserts and mountains and caves and holes in the ground.

³⁹ And all these, having gained approval through their faith, did not receive what was promised, ⁴⁰ because God had provided something better for us, so that apart from us they would not be made perfect.

One of the most fascinating things about Hebrews 11, especially verse 39, is that all these people gained God's approval but died awaiting the fulfillment of their promise. But that isn't the end of their story. The conclusion of Hebrews 11 is actually found in the next chapter, Hebrews 12:1-2. It says to "fix our eyes on Jesus". Let me come back to this in a moment. Paul repeatedly emphasized in his writings that our life exists, to some degree or another, "in the middle." However, as people of God in whom lives the "Spirit of the AGE TO COME," we are continually guided by a voice within us Who lives presently in our future. This is why Paul could offer his brief treatise on life "in the middle"— *"...we are afflicted in every way, but not crushed; perplexed, but not despairing; persecuted, but not forsaken; struck down, but not destroyed..."* (2 Corinthians 4:8-10).

"In the middle" is where you gain the clearest understanding of your beginning...giving you FAITH for an end that remains yet unseen! The middle provides you with perspective on the facts of your past and how you arrived at your present...but those facts are meant to birth the faith it will take to get you from your present to God's glorious future for you! Therefore, the middle is the place where your deepest convictions are formed that declare, "Lord, You didn't bring me this far to leave me here. Holy Spirit, lead me on to my future!"

> "In the middle" is where you gain the clearest understanding of your beginning...giving you FAITH for an end that remains yet unseen!

- Living life "in the middle" may lead you to build something for an outcome that only you have seen. Just ask Noah!

- Living life "in the middle" may lead you to erect altars of sacrifice, having left the comfort zone and familiarity of family and your hometown. Just ask Abraham!

- Living life "in the middle" may prove that the greatest asset gained is the staff you have to lean on—evidence of having wrestled with God and man and having overcome but be sure...people will line up to partake of that victorious anointing. Just ask Jacob!

- Living life "in the middle" may cause others to be jealous, sell you out, lie about you, ignore you, forget you, and leave you in a dungeon to rot. Just ask Joseph!

- Living life "in the middle" gives people a window to the future, enabling them to consider the reproach of being anointed as greater than possessing the wealth and success of this world. Just ask Moses!

- Living life "in the middle" will lead to acts of great faith beyond your status in life, only to help you discover that you have gained great victories in battles you were just hoping to survive. Just ask Gideon!

- Living life "in the middle" tells us that there is always an opportunity for redemption, no matter how badly we may have failed. Just ask Samson!

- Living life "in the middle" provides amazing opportunities to do amazingly stupid stuff and yet find that God has not abandoned us. Just ask Jephthah or David!

- Living life "in the middle" will provide an occasion for you to be the next obvious meal for hungry lions only to discover that God has removed you from the menu. Just ask Daniel!

- Living life "in the middle" will lead you to abandon idolatry, selfish ambition, and the quest to be awesome. It may lead you through life's darkest valleys, only for you to discover that the darkness cannot consume you because of the glorious light of Christ that saves you. Just ask Buck Marshall! Oh, wait! That's me!!

- Living life "in the middle" may lead you down a path of aloneness, often being misunderstood, falsely accused, and maligned in every way. In a very real sense, it may lead you to being unjustly crucified. Just ask Jesus!

You will discover that God crafted a "life in the middle" for Himself...He called it incarnation. Therefore...fixing our eyes on Jesus...the Author and Perfector of our faith...Who for the joy set before Him...ran "to the middle" ...a cross...and made a public spectacle of all principalities and powers that tried to shame Him!

Life is full of people who have wasted "in the middle" complaining, giving up, or simply refusing to press on. I urge you - do not be one of those people! The choice is yours! IT IS NOT OVER - you're just in the middle of your story!

CHAPTER 10

Thank You

T HOSE TWO WORDS COULDN'T possibly convey the gratefulness I have for the following people. I owe them a debt, each in their own way, for different reasons, and at various levels. Nevertheless, I am forever thankful for all the parts they played, not only in getting this book published, but also in getting through the years this book touches on. Therefore, the following paragraphs are about the creation of this book and the path or journey that led to it. It certainly must be said that I could never thank everyone individually or adequately. But please know that for everyone who helped in big and small ways...I am grateful to each of you from the bottom of my heart.

First and foremost, thank you God. You deserve all glory, power, and praise. Worthy is The Lamb. I exalt You. The cords of death surrounded me, I was overcome by trouble and sorrow, but then I cried unto The Lord. And YOU saved me! I am so glad You not only called me, equipped me, and sent me, but also never gave up on me. Without You, Jesus, I don't know what I'd do. I love You...I love You...I love You.

Second only to the Lord, I am thankful for my precious bride. Thank you for marrying, putting up with, and believing in me. We have walked in high and lowly places together, known what it is to abound and be abased...but no matter how difficult it got...you stayed with me...continued to seek Him...and remained faithful to the call of God. You are simply incredible. Thank you for walking each and every one of these steps with me. Beautiful, wise, passionate, gifted, fierce in the Spirit, and anointed of the Lord...you're just simply the greatest person I know. I love you with all my heart.

To my children, Caroline and Jonathan...thank you. Much of this journey impacted you both in different ways. I am so glad that instead of becoming bitter, you both have taken up the call of ministry and are giving yourselves to spreading the Gospel and walking in a Holy Yes to The Lord. I am in awe as I watch you, Caroline, sing, dance, preach to hundreds, or sit and talk to one person for hours about the revelation God is giving you in His Word. Thank you for loving me through the journey and being my little girl. Jonathan, I love watching you walk up to strangers and pray for them...witness to them...or lead others to do the same, whether we are in Times Square or Home Depot...you seem to always have a heart to connect people to Jesus. Thank you for being my travel buddy. I love you both.

There would be no book if it were not for the late Dr. David Ford. He encouraged me to get my doctorate and made a way for me to do so, and out of that came this book. I have converted it from a doctoral project to what you have read here, but without that man of faith...this wouldn't have happened. I am so grateful that God sent him into my life at just the right time. I love how Dr. Ford truly walked by faith and not by sight. I miss you, brother...but remain grateful for your influence, I feel it still.

Thank you, Pastors Tom and Brenda Sterbens, for who you are and for being present in my life. I don't know what we would have done without your voice in some really dark hours. Pastor Tom, you have always been one who can see through the chaos and find the through-line of the Word. I am so grateful for your voice, your integrity, your influence, your help, and your love. I love you both.

There were some companions in Ennis during those times. Some came for seasons, and I am grateful to them, but there were a few throughout the entire journey that remained steadfast in their care and love for me and my family, and I just wouldn't have made it without them. Clint Sublett, you are one of the most generous people I have ever met. Your encouragement and sense of hope were a beacon of light to me. Glenn Hobbs...what a mighty man of God. Quiet and unassuming, yet when you spoke...everyone listened. You were a pillar in that church and in my life. Thank you for your strength. Debbie Lynch, you were always kind and met us with compassion. Thank you for that...it was more powerful than you know. Rev. Markus T. Sallie, you are my brother from another mother. Your support, love, and honor for me and my family were like a healing balm, and your presence in our lives is non-negotiable. You are one of the very few people around whom I feel completely relaxed and safe. Thank you for that gift. And thank you for being my friend. Bill and Suzanne Rhoten, I don't think my kids would have made it without you two. That theater of yours became a city of refuge and a hospital for their soul. You met them with no judgment, saw not just their gifts but also their hearts...and loved them like they were your own. For a man who didn't really like working with kids...Bill, you sure became committed to Caroline and Jonathan as well as a puddle of tears, a constant hugger, and the author of more than one mischievous adventure with them. Thank you, Suzanne, for pointing them to the Word and prayer. To you both, I am forever in your debt. I love you.

Richard Henderson...you sent me on a quest that changed me, then Rhea, then our marriage. You and Paige became voices crying in our wilderness...prepare the way of the Lord! With tears as I write this...Thank you. Thank you for getting us the cabin in Colorado next to the river, which led to the encounter that changed my life. Thank you for always being a voice that points out God's fingerprints that elude most yet remain obvious to you. You are a true man of God, and I am thankful for you and Paige.

Thank you, Jim and Judy Marshall...my mom and dad. You kept our kids every Friday night so we could steal away for a few hours for date night, you gave us money when we were broke, you prayed life into us when we were down, you loved us when the battle was hot, tended our wounds, and sowed into our ministry in more ways than I can count. Mama, your prayers sustained us. You are a fierce prayer warrior, and I love you. Dad, I will never forget you calling me when I was ready to throw in the towel. In my next book, I will tell that story, but suffice it to say that you told me not to give up and then ended with a Melville quote you knew I'd know. "We be whaling men or no?!" I have never forgotten that. It is a reminder that I am a preacher of the Gospel, and that's what I am and what I will continue to do....no matter what. Thank you for your strength. I love you.

My sister Michelle, thank you for becoming my friend. Thank you for sowing into us, being the world's greatest aunt, loving our kids, giving us the gift of laughter when we needed it most, and praying for us through it all. I love you, sis.

Bishop Tim Hill, you have been a friend to me in more ways than I can count, and I am so thankful for you. You have been so gracious in sharing your time, your wisdom, and your experience with me. Thank you for writing the forward, but mainly for being my friend.

Bryan Cutshall, you have been such an encouragement to me, especially in writing this book. Thank you for pointing me in the right direction, giving me some idea of how to do this, offering names of people that could help, and being a sounding board. Thank you for taking the time to do all that. I appreciate you!

Crystal Smith, thank you for being just an awesome editor. You graciously took what I had written and helped tweak it into this manuscript. You are a blessing, and I appreciate the work you did and especially the encouragement you offered.

Thank you to my publisher, Tony Colson. You reached out to me several years ago and offered to help make this happen, but the truth was, I just wasn't ready. But when I called you again, you sprang into action and made a way for me to get this into people's hands. You have been patient and a constant voice saying, "You can do it!" I appreciate everything you did...especially ensuring my book stayed mine in content, look, and ownership.

I want to extend a special thank you to Bishop Raymond Culpepper, Dr. Fred Garmon, Renee Talley, Rev. Dawn Lipsey, and Bishop Tony Stewart for their endorsements of this book. I love each of you.

Pastor Cary and Brenda Anderson, thank you for sowing into this book and providing the opportunity to get it published. At the time, you didn't know why the Lord had you do that, but it is why you now hold this book in your hand. And, more importantly, I am thankful for you, Cary. You are a blessing to my life.

To everyone who prayed, encouraged, gave of their time to love on me, lifted my heavy hands, believed in me when I didn't believe in myself, sowed into our ministry when I didn't know if we could make it, laughed with me when I wanted to cry, and stood with me while others walked away...you are heroes one and all. Right in the middle of my story...you were salt and light...vessels of hope...hands of help...feet of Jesus...and you ushered me and my family through it all...to the other side. Yeah...thank you doesn't quite cover it. So I will simply add a heartfelt God bless you...I love you all.

Note From The Author

This note wasn't even my idea. It was my editor's. Yet, the more I thought about it, the more I sensed the Holy Spirit was in it. You see, while this book was written primarily for Christian believers and especially those in ministry, I cannot help but hope that it may have gotten into the hands of someone who either is not a believer or once was but has turned away from the path of Christ once walked. If you have read this book and the Holy Spirit has touched your heart...you may feel stirred...it is the Holy Spirit drawing you to Jesus. It is the voice of God encouraging you to believe in Jesus Christ and entrust your life to Him. Or it may be that He is urging you to come back home and allow Him to heal the wounds that turned you away. If you are that person, I have written this note just for you. If you received Jesus as your Lord and Savior in the process of reading this book, or rededicated your life to Him, I would love to hear from you! Please contact me at the email address below so that I can celebrate with you on your new life in Christ. I promise I will personally read each one.

Dr. Buck Marshall
Email: inthemiddleofyourstory@gmail.com

Bibliography

Baker Books. *A Walk Thru the Life of Joseph*. Grand Rapids: Baker Publishing Group, 2009.

Bonhoeffer, Dietrich. *Temptation*. New York: Macmillan Publishing Co., Collier Books, 1953.

Brant, Roxanne. *Ministering to the Lord*. New Kensington: Whitaker Press, 1973.

Chambers, Oswald. *Not Knowing Whither: The Steps of Abraham's Faith*. Grand Rapids: Discovery House, 2015.

Collins, Kenneth J. *A Real Christian*. Nashville: Abington Press, 1999.

Cutshall, Bryan. *Your Promised Land Awaits.* New Kensington: Whitaker House, 2008.

Deere, Jack. *Surprised by the Power of His Spirit.* Grand Rapids: Zondervan, 1993.

Deere, Jack. *Surprised by the Voice of God.* Grand Rapids: Zondervan, 1996.

Ford, David. *Activating the Power of God.* Birmingham: Evangelistic Messengers Association, 2009.

Gene Getz, Joseph. *Overcoming Obstacles through Faithfulness.* Nashville: Broadman & Holman, Publishers, 1996.

Hayford, Jack W. *Prayer is Invading the Impossible.* Alachua: Bridge Logos, 1977.

Hillman, Os. *The Joseph Calling: 6 Stages to Discover, Navigate, and Fulfill Your Purpose.* Racine: BroadStreet Publishing Group LLC, 2017.

Proodian, John David. *Accelerated Healing.* Shippensburg: Destiny Image Publishers, 2018.

Smith, Sr., Robert E. *Elimination of Erroneous Distinctions.* Little Rock: Total Outreach Ministries, 1995.

Sterbens, Tom. *Issues in Contemporary Pentecostalism* - Kindle Edition by Arrington, French L. Religion & Spirituality Kindle Ebooks @ Amazon.Com, 2012.

Swindoll, Charles R. *Joseph.* Nashville: Thomas Nelson, 1998.

Uppal, Steve. *The Burning Ones.* Barham Court: River Publishing, 2013.

ABOUT THE AUTHOR

Buck Marshall has devoted over thirty years to preaching the Gospel of Jesus Christ, serving in various roles such as youth pastor, senior pastor, and evangelist. Earning degrees in world missions, family ministry, and biblical studies, he has personally traveled to over seventy countries, sharing the Gospel, building churches, starting Bible schools, while seeking to embody the love of Jesus in every interaction. An ordained bishop, he has recently been appointed as a National Evangelist for the Church of God (Cleveland, TN). Buck has been married to Rhea, the love of his life, for 27 years, and together they have two children, Caroline and Jonathan.

Endnotes

1. Jack Deere, *Surprised by the Voice of God* (Grand Rapids: Zondervan, 1996), 26-27.

2. Kenneth J. Collins, *A Real Christian* (Nashville: Abington Press, 1999), 150-151.

3. Baker Books, *A Walk Thru the Life of Joseph* (Grand Rapids: Baker Publishing Group, 2009), 11-12.

4. Baker Books, *A Walk Thru the Life of Joseph* (Grand Rapids: Baker Publishing Group, 2009), 14-15.

5. Robert E. Smith, Sr., *Elimination of Erroneous Distinctions* (Little Rock: Total Outreach Ministries, 1995), 5.

6. David Ford, *Activating the Power of God* (Birmingham: Evangelistic Messengers Association, 2009), 59-60.

7. Os Hillman, *The Joseph Calling: 6 Stages to Discover, Navigate, and Fulfill Your Purpose* (Racine: BroadStreet Publishing Group LLC, 2017), 50.

8. Oswald Chambers, *Not Knowing Whither: The Steps of Abraham's Faith* (Grand Rapids: Discovery House, 2015), Google e-book.

9. Dietrich Bonhoeffer, *Temptation* (New York: Macmillan Publishing Co., Collier Books, 1953), 116–117.

10. Charles R. Swindoll, *Joseph* (Nashville: Thomas Nelson, 1998), 22.

11. Os Hillman, *The Joseph Calling: 6 Stages to Discover, Navigate, and Fulfill Your Purpose* (Racine: BroadStreet Publishing Group LLC, 2017), 52-53.

12. John David Proodian, *Accelerated Healing* (Shippensburg: Destiny Image Publishers, 2018), 29.

13. Baker Books, *A Walk Thru the Life of Joseph* (Grand Rapids: Baker Publishing Group, 2009), 15-16.

14. Sterbens, Tom. *Issues in Contemporary Pentecostalism* - Kindle Edition by Arrington, French L. Religion & Spirituality Kindle Ebooks @ Amazon.Com, Chapter 12.

15. Sterbens, Tom. *Issues in Contemporary Pentecostalism* - Kindle Edition by Arrington, French L. Religion & Spirituality Kindle Ebooks @ Amazon.Com, Chapter 12.

16. Baker Books, *A Walk Thru the Life of Joseph* (Grand Rapids: Baker Publishing Group, 2009), 28-29.

17. Charles R. Swindoll, *Joseph* (Nashville: Thomas Nelson, 1998), 58-59.

18. Jack Deere, *Surprised by the Power of His Spirit* (Grand Rapids: Zondervan, 1993), 185.

19. Steve Uppal, *The Burning Ones* (Barham Court: River Publishing, 2013), 57-58.

20. Bryan Cutshall, *Your Promised Land Awaits.* (New Kensington: Whitaker House, 2008), 426.

21. Os Hillman, *The Joseph Calling: 6 Stages to Discover, Navigate, and Fulfill Your Purpose* (Racine: BroadStreet Publishing Group LLC, 2017), 24.

22. Charles R. Swindoll, *Joseph* (Nashville: Thomas Nelson, 1998), 62-63; 70-71.

23. Roxanne Brant, *Ministering to the Lord* (New Kensington: Whitaker Press, 1973), 56.

24. Joseph Gene Getz, *Overcoming Obstacles through Faithfulness* (Nashville: Broadman & Holman, Publishers, 1996), 108.

25. Jack W. Hayford, *Prayer is Invading the Impossible* (Alachua: Bridge Logos, 1977), 196-197.

26. Baker Books, *A Walk Thru the Life of Joseph* (Grand Rapids: Baker Publishing Group, 2009), 69.

27. Baker Books, *A Walk Thru the Life of Joseph* (Grand Rapids: Baker Publishing Group, 2009), 69.

BUCKANDRHEA.COM

Book Dr. Marshall For Your Next Speaking Engagment